Shop, Save, and Share

ELLIE KAY

BETHANY HOUSE PUBLISHERS
MINNEAPOLIS, MINNESOTA 55438

Published by Bethany House Publishers
A Ministry of Bethany Fellowship International
11400 Hampshire Avenue South
Minneapolis, Minnesota 55438
www.bethanyhouse.com

Printed in the United States of America by
Bethany Press International, Minneapolis, Minnesota 55438

ISBN 0–7642–2083–7

This book is dedicated to my "Beloved"—
you are exceedingly abundantly above all
I could ask for or dream of.
And to the children
who made me a half-wit—
Daniel, Philip, Bethany, Jonathan, and Joshua.
You are my delight.

ELLIE KAY is founder and author of *Shop, Save, and Share* Seminars and a gifted speaker and writer. She is a graduate of Colorado Christian University with a degree in the management of human resources. She and her husband, Bob, a career fighter pilot with the U.S. Air Force, have five children and make their home in New York State.

If you wish to contact Ellie Kay for speaking engagements or to conduct her seminar, she can be reached at:

Ellie Kay
PO Box 229
Ft. Drum, NY 13603

e-mail: halfwit5@juno.com

Acknowledgments

As every author will tell you, there are lots of people behind the scenes who contribute to a book. I'll start at the beginning.

Cheryl Shelton has been a cheerleader of mine way back when *Shop, Save, and Share* was only "Shopping Tips" in a women's meeting at Believer's Bible Church. Thank you, Cheryl, for believing in me when I didn't believe in myself. She plugged my seminar to every listening ear and eventually helped me find Becky Freeman again.

Becky wears many hats. Not only is she a bestselling author of seven books, she's also been a wonderful agent, editor, speaker, mom, and humorist. (The last two hats are best worn together.) I want to thank Becky for her generous help in taking this novice through the million and one hurdles in publishing a book. Thank you, Becky. This book couldn't have happened without you.

To Kevin Johnson, senior editor of nonfiction at Bethany House, thank you for taking a risk on a new, unknown author. To Steve Laube, the editor of this book, you've managed to keep your sense of humor from the beginning; your professionalism is much appreciated.

A special acknowledgment goes to my publicist at Bethany House, Jeanne Mikkelson. Thank you for your patience and hard work; I don't take you for granted.

There were a few people with tremendous vision who saw the potential *Shop, Save, and Share* had to help U.S. Air Force families. Major

General Bruce Carlson, Lenn Furrow, and Judy Drews, thank you for taking on the project to bring the video of this seminar to air force families via the Air Force Aid Society. Families all over the world have been enriched by your vision.

I'd also like to thank Major General Lawson and Gloria Magruder for their enthusiasm in bringing this program to U.S. Army families. Your genuine concern for people and your kindness are evident in all you do.

To my kindred spirit, Madeline Brazell, thank you for encouraging me to pursue a dream and to despise not the day of small beginnings. Your prayers, notes, and words of hope helped make the vision become reality.

To my "Three Musketeers": my Beloved, Brenda Taylor, and Loretta Grapes, who have helped me fight the battles in the process of this book, I thank you. My Beloved, you've given me soil, sunshine, and refreshing water to bloom where I am planted. This book would be meaningless without you to share it with. Your encouragement for me to "be all that I can be" has inspired me to heights I thought reserved for those more accomplished than I. Thank you for your faithfulness.

Brenda, my garage-sale buddy, bosom friend, and great encourager—you've stuck by me closer than a brother and built me up when others tore down. Your steady stream of communication has been a source of nourishment as you feed my soul with God's mercy and grace.

Loretta, your humor and wisdom have carried me throughout the years. Your disorganization complements my order, and when I'm wound too tight, you release that spring with your wit and honesty.

To our closest family members, Steve and Debby Kay, we thank you for being the "California Kays" and for providing some consistency in our separation from family. To Milt and Dorothy Kay, thank you for your prayers for the boys all those years ago.

Moving in the military means constant separation from parents and grandparents. But God has been faithful to provide. Marveen Thomas and Pauline Parker have been those grannies to the babies and moms to Bob and me. Marveen, thanks for those notes, cards, and cartoons—you're always thinking of others. You have shown me repeatedly how much you care. Your godliness is an example to young women. I pray that one day, *many* years from now, I'm half the grandma you are!

Pauline, thank you for your prayers and perspective—when you pray, God listens! Your counsel has helped me keep the faith, and your generosity in love has kept the well of my heart full.

Elke Slinkerd, thanks for letting me share the day-by-day developments on our five-mile walks. Your genuine interest has been a source of strength.

There's a special prayer team that has been faithful behind the scenes to support our family in the drama of this publication. I'd like to thank you and list my "team" by name. These are the people who have maintained weekly if not daily contact, and lifted us up in prayer when we were "plumb tired." Blessings to Pastor Jack and Sharon Brock, Robyn Brown, the Coxes, the Davenports, Karen Eckerle, Ellie Fondren, the Hoeves, the Keating family, Gayla McDougal, Jennifer Mattison, Jill and Darren Mingear, Jessica Nichols, The Sierts, The Smathers, Mark and Diane Thomas, Carla Thompson, the Trevillions, and Jayne Warner.

I also thank my parents, Rodger and Paquita Rawleigh, for instilling in me at a young age the value of hard work and perseverance. I come from a long line of penny pinchers.

Last, but certainly not least, I want to remember two little girls, Missy and Mandy, who aren't so little anymore—but still just as precious as ever. My heart has never forgotten you.

CONTENTS

Foreword

The phone call was unexpected—and a delight. "Becky?" the voice on the other end of the line asked.

"Yes," I replied.

"You may not remember me, but back in the '70s you and I went to the same church—I'm Ellie Kay now, but I used to be Ellie Rawleigh."

"Little Ellie?" I asked in surprise. "Of course I remember you! You were sweet and beautiful and kind of quiet—"

"Well, I've kind of outgrown the 'quiet' part. I've got five kids now, I'm married to a fighter pilot, and my life is a lot like you describe yours to be in *Worms in My Tea....*"

Our catch-up conversation went on for almost an hour, and by the time I hung up the phone, I realized with wonder: *Little Ellie has grown up.*

Her family stories were so funny, but she was also wise and poised. She'd had her share of heartaches, but she had chosen to find joy. Her love for Christ and her family was evident in the stories she shared. When she told me about her *Shop, Save, and Share* seminars and the book she was writing, I knew that even though Ellie called herself a half-wit, she was the kind of gal who would never do anything halfway. I was pleased that she entrusted me to serve as her agent, saying, "Anyway, Becky, the outcome is really in God's hands." Never once, through the ups and downs that come with finding a publishing home, did she waver from that firm conviction.

Eventually my husband, Scott, and I drove to a nearby campground to meet the Kay family in person—the whole bunch of them. They happened to be passing through our small Texas town on the way to their new military home in New York. (That will tell you how many miles they had ahead of them.)

We arrived an hour and a half later than planned (having taken a few wrong country turns) and I was suffering from jumbo-sized PMS. When I saw Ellie—relaxed and beautiful, walking out of the camper—I wondered what she would think about this very untogether-feeling author. (People sometimes have the idea that authors float above the mundane things of life—like wrong turns and severe PMS.)

I needn't have worried—Ellie was warm and welcoming, and I felt within minutes that we'd been friends for a long, long time. We also shared a passion for hot coffee and dark chocolate—and at the moment, I needed a good dose of both. The fellows graciously agreed to watch the kids while Ellie and I stole away for some girl talk at a local café.

As we gathered up our things to leave, I glanced over at Scott, whose arms were brimming with hugging Kay children. They were sweet, exuberant kids—the kind that love you just because you are there. Bob was intelligent and kind, with a mischievous twinkle in his eyes and a love for his bride that was both rare and beautiful to behold. He literally beamed his pride at all Ellie had brought to his life, at her enthusiasm in helping to stretch the family budget, and at her "blossoming" into an informative and hilarious professional speaker and writer. And yes, Bob and Ellie really do address each other by the endearing term "Beloved." (Which I think is a stroke of genius. I mean, how can you yell at someone you are calling Beloved?)

It is with a heart full of enthusiasm that I invite you into the pages of this book. Not only will you be inspired to shop your way to saving and sharing—I think you'll also find yourself falling in love with Ellie. Ellie the Half-Witted Mother of Five (as she calls herself). Ellie the Faithful, Funny, Chocolate-Covered Friend. Ellie the Beloved. Not only is Ellie called Beloved by her husband, but she is also called Beloved by a Savior who means everything to her. May you discover, through Ellie's winsome wisdom, that you, too, are beloved of God.

Becky Freeman
Greenville, Texas, 1998

Introduction

I didn't plan eight moves in the last ten years, or five babies in seven years. There are lots of unplanned events in my life. I never dreamed of writing a book while simultaneously running a business and caring for children ages nine to one (with a military husband who is gone more than he's home).

How could a distracted, not-always-together mom have the ability to write a book? I can barely remember my children's names. They are Daniel, Philip, uh...Bethany, Josh...no, there's Jonathan, and *then* Joshua. Do you see what I mean?

There was a time when I remembered things without help and even spoke in complete sentences. I believe my brain capacity began to diminish when the children started coming along—one right after the other. Then I had to think for my kids and had no brain cells left for myself. For example, there are doctor's appointments, sports practices, school projects, Awana nights, clothing sizes, and on and on—multiplied by five.

On top of my children's commitments, I have to remember a few items for my fighter-pilot husband. He can fly multimillion dollar jets but can't remember the highway exit *without my help*. He can locate a target from 100 miles out—but can't find his other black sock.

Finally, there are the activities to remember for myself: seminars, speaking engagements, school schedules, air force functions, church commitments, family services volunteer days, etc.—it's no wonder I have half a brain.

Consequently, I'm the self-proclaimed "Half-Witted Mother of Five." You may think it's a funny way to look at myself, but humor has nothing to do with it—survival does. There's a very important lesson to be learned regarding eight moves and five babies. One of two things would inevitably happen. I could either learn to view life in a funny way or end up on a funny *farm*.

Now that you know my major flaw (limited gray matter), I might as well let you know a minor flaw. You must promise not to tell anyone. Come closer and I'll whisper it. Okay—*I have ugly feet.* Shhhh! *Please* don't tell anyone. After all, it's a personal problem. All those years of having babies made my feet somewhat deformed. Before I had Daniel I wore a size seven shoe—with each baby I gained half a shoe size, and now I wear a nine. Also, all those years of running after the kids have taken their toll on my poor feetsies. The good news is: I usually hide them in shoes.

If a half-wit, who speaks in fragmented sentences, melts the baby's pacifier in the oven, and has ugly feet can *write* this book, then you can surely *do* what it says to do.

Throughout the following pages, you'll meet our five children and see that we're just an average family—a family like yours (well, maybe not exactly like yours). You'll meet Daniel, our oldest, a responsible and bright firstborn with a penchant for playing by the rules and an insight into life that is amazing. Philip, our kind and sensitive second son, provides an endless supply of honest commentaries on life—both in season and out. Bethany, the only girl, is her papa's delight and her mama's joy. We call her "Bunny" because she hops from heart to heart. Finally, you'll meet the mischievous brothers Jonathan and Joshua, whose antics are enough to drive a half-wit to the farm. Jonathan has a soft side, earning him the nickname "Sweetpea." Joshua, on the other hand, is also known as "Conan, the Baby Barbarian." If he were our first—he would have been our last. Every one of these children is a keeper.

Believe it or not, my babies helped write this book. They've unknowingly provided a backdrop to the drama on family savings. There is no other money savings book on the market like *Shop, Save, and Share*. What makes this approach so unique? In Section One, *Shop*, there is a step-by-step method of grocery shopping that is simple and systematic. Finally, someone is here to show you how to easily organize your coupons into significant savings. I've invested ten years of experience into the development of this system of grocery shopping. This approach was also developed through input from people like you throughout the years. The result is a method so refined, it only takes an hour and a half a week to save *big* bucks.

How much do I save our family? I'm glad you asked. My *average* receipt is $120 before coupons and only $50 (or less) after coupons. Our family's grocery budget is $200 a month, and I often come in under budget. A typical family of seven in the United States (with children our children's ages) spent $10,388 in 1997 for *food alone*. We included cleansers, toiletries, and diapers in our annual budget of $2,400. Consequently, I saved our family well over $8,000 last year. On top of that incredible savings, I was able to give 100 bags (or $1,000 worth) of food to those in need.

This savings is achieved through coupons from your local Sunday paper with no other gimmicks or sleight-of-hand tricks. The other Coupon Queens you've seen on television (who pay $3 for $300 worth of groceries) are illusions—they're not realistic for the average shopper.

These women organize the televised shop for months, they don't do it on a weekly basis. As a matter of fact, over half of the products from their grand shopping spree are bought with coupons secured through refunds from the manufacturer. This book is not a production for the camera—it's a way of life.

Section Two, *Save,* serves as a handy reference guide. It covers money-saving tips on everything from credit cards to clothing. You'll discover painless ways to cut costs on entertainment and energy. (First, I have to *find* some energy, then maybe I can learn to *save* energy.)

Section Three, *Share,* focuses on the foundations of sharing, mixing the philosophical with the practical. You'll learn how to do everything a little better—from busting stress to simplifying life.

When I was researching this book, I met a lot of Coupon Queens via a ProQuest program at our local library. There were photos in magazine articles showing them standing next to their warehouse full of groceries. Most of these women had enough goods to open a mini-store! I mean, who needs twenty-five bottles of dishwashing soap? *I* don't even do that many dishes! That brings me to the single factor that makes this book different from any you've read.

Shop, Save, and Share emphasizes the *Share.* I don't have a HUGE stockpile of groceries (there are only six bottles of dishwashing soap under my sink). Instead, I encourage people to give food away to others in need. Consequently, my mini grocery store is at the local homeless shelter. My groceries are on the shelves of the women's shelter and the community food pantry. That extra dishwashing soap is washing dishes at a church soup kitchen that is helping to feed the hungry in our town.

There are no gimmicks involved in this book, nothing to buy or sell. Everything you need to start your savings program is here. All that's required is a teachable spirit and some scissors.

Shop

Rent-A-Yenta

Tips to Resisting Impulse Buying

My husband was off flying a jet somewhere over the Middle East during the last days of Desert Storm. I was back home managing a storm of my own: a three-year-old, an eighteen-month-old, and a newborn. To win the war I would battle that morning, I knew I had to have my troops up by sunrise—for I'd discovered the best time to attack the grocery store is by dawn's early light.

If you have never been to the grocery store before 7:00 A.M., I recommend it. Meeting interesting characters (the kind who are out shopping before sane people have had their first sip of coffee) makes it worth the extra effort. I do need to offer a small warning to mothers of multiple preschoolers, however. Early shoppers don't usually have children at home, and I've found they love nothing more than helping out half-witted mothers with a cart full of kids.

On this particular morning, I drove to the store, stuffed my three kids in the cart, and wheeled my entourage toward the produce section. Before I'd squeezed the first nectarine, a woman behind me offered a suggestion, spoken in low, "just-between-us-girls" tones.

"Honey," she began, "you really ought to remove your purse from that grocery cart handle and strap it on your body somewhere. Someone could just come right by and steal it."

"But the purse strap is tied to the cart," I protested. My advisor's eyebrows shot up under her bangs, obviously unsatisfied with my reply.

"Yeah," she replied knowingly, "but there are people who walk around with scissors, just waiting to cut the straps on a purse like that. It happened to my daughter."

Who was I to argue? It was hard to imagine a scissors-toting purse thief lurking behind the rutabagas, but I suppose one can't be too careful. Bob and I have a standard answer (usually given through clenched teeth) for unsolicited wisdom. As I watched the woman shuffle indignantly off toward the aisles, her purse strap tightly wound around her waist, I called out, "Thank you for your input!"

As I rounded the corner near an Oreo cookie display, I nearly ran over a Yenta. Yes, a Yenta. As in "little Jewish matchmaker." Like the one from *Fiddler on the Roof*. She was diminutive—two inches shy of five feet— but her expression was imposing enough to make up for what she lacked in height. She wore her gray hair wrapped in a scarf and, in spite of her thick New York accent, she even sounded like Yenta.

"Oh, my goodness, oh, my gosh!" the woman exclaimed, smacking her forehead with her open palm as she carried on a conversation with someone who wasn't there.

"I can't believe what I see heyah." She pointed at me but directed her question to the invisible person behind her. "Can you believe this?" I wondered if I should acknowledge the invisible person with a nod or something.

Yenta squinted her eyes in deep concern, patting my arm as she spoke. "Can you believe this? Did you knowah? Did you knowah that you could put yah back out doing that?" Turning, she quizzed her alter ego.

"Can she put her back out or what? I ask you. Pulling those carts full of food and those kids?"

For once, I was speechless. No matter—my newfound mentor was quick to fill in the silence. "You could put yah back out, that's what. They have people heah that can push those carts for yah." Way down the aisle, she spied a stock boy unloading boxes in the dairy section. Not a problem for Yenta. She stood on her toes (which made her four-foot, eleven-inches tall) and shouted, "Hey youwah! Yeah, you mistah! I don't mean yah mutha', I don't mean yah fatha', I mean YOUWAH! COME HEAYAH NOW!"

The startled stock boy came running as she scolded him. "Did yah know that this woman is going to put her back out?" Turning again, she asked her invisible friend, "Is she going to put her back out or what?" Looking back to the bewildered teenager, she stomped her foot. "Yes, she's going to put her back out and where will yah be then, I ASK YOU? You'll be in the poorhouse, that's what. She'll put her back out, sue your store, and you'll be out of a job that's what. Will he be out of a job, or what? So ya'd bettah push her cart to the check-out and ya'd bettah do it NOW!"

Not wanting to lose his job or take on a lawsuit, the boy immediately went to work pushing my cart of groceries. Overwhelmed by the entire experience, I stared at Yenta, opened my mouth to say something, and again, nothing came out.

She helped me. "I know what yah thinking.... Yes, I know what yah thinking. Do we know—" she turned, "what she's thinking?"

She struck the pose of a saint, one hand gently resting in the palm of the other. "You're thinking that ya'd like to say thank you. No need to say thanks, I do things like this because I love people. A poor widow woman all alone in de world, but I'm always thinking of others. Yes, I love people, that's what."

Finally, I found my voice and stammered, "Thank you for your input."

As she walked away, I could faintly hear her asking, "Do we love people or what? I ask you..."

She girds herself with strength, and makes her arms strong.
Proverbs 31:17

You may meet plenty of people anxious to give you well-meaning advice in the grocery store. You may even have to exercise a tremendous amount of inner strength, grit your teeth, and say, "Thank you for your input."

Another area in which you'll need self-control is in the area of impulse buying. Americans waste thousands of dollars each year on spontaneous purchases. Here's a survival guide based on research and marketing savvy that could help you leave the store with extra change in your wallet.

Tips to Resisting Impulse Buying
Whaddaya Do If Yah Don't Have a Yenta?

Throughout the book I will provide a list of tips at the end of each chapter. These tips will help you master destructive buying patterns. If you apply only one tip each week from each of this book's three sections, you'll experience *significant* savings within a couple of months.

Just Say No

As you may have guessed, marketing experts depend on our impulse-buying tendencies. They place the most expensive items at eye level and the bargains on the upper and lower shelves. If you're as short as Yenta, you might notice the additional products on the lower shelves. If not, then look high and low for the best deals.

Go Ahead and Smell the Flowers, Just Don't Pay Big Bucks for Them

The floral, bakery, and gift sections are directly in the main path of shoppers navigating their way from the entrance to the aisles. Like a toll bridge from fairy-tale fame, you have to cross these sections to get to the other side. But you don't have to pay a toll! There are many ways to save money on flowers, baked goods, and gifts, which I'll share later on. For now, steer your cart on fast-forward through these money-draining traps.

You Think Better With a Full Stomach

You're less likely to splurge on unneeded items if you go to the store when you're not hungry.

Absence Makes the Heart Grow Fonder

If possible, leave the babies at home or with a friend. Sans kids, I find my concentration is better and I'm less likely to give in to *their* desire to buy on impulse. Marketing organizations are smart—they put all the kid stuff right on eye level with the ankle biters. Another added benefit—without your entourage, you're out of the store faster.

Make a List and Don't Leave Home Without It!

It's a known fact among consumer researchers that people who shop with a list (and stick to it) consistently spend less. We'll see helpful ideas about the specific content and structure of that list later on in the book.

"New and Improved" Does Not Always Mean New and Improved

The food industry spends $6 billion a year in fancy packaging and compelling displays. Their purpose? To weaken sales resistance in shoppers. To boost sales, old products are often given a face-lift through a new package. Evaluate every item to determine whether it's a good buy.

Ignore the gimmicks.

Make Your House Your Home—Not the Store

I enjoy shopping, but it's not my life. I go to the store no more than once a week. Overexposure in the supermarket makes you susceptible to impulse buying. If you calculate all those little trips, you'll find they add up to big bucks. Shop once a week and you'll save time, money, *and* gas.

Don't Fight the Crowds

The least busy times at the store are Thursday evenings and early Saturday mornings. My friend Cindy shops at the same store every Saturday morning and has made friends with the early shift, who look forward to her regular trips. Without the pressure of a crowded store, you'll spend less money and pull out less hair.

Leave the Plastic and Paper at Home

Take cash to the grocery store and leave your credit cards, checkbook, and IOUs at home. This will help limit you to only those things you need and force you to stay within your budget. I know I would rather subject myself to Chinese water torture than find myself at the check-out with too many groceries and too little cash!

Bonus Tip: Shop the Loss Leaders

A loss leader is an advertised item designed to entice buyers into a store. Oftentimes, the store will lose money on these products, but they'll make up the difference when Aunt Harriet comes to their store for her entire week's worth of shopping. It's a marketing risk that's proven to be a good investment for grocery and retail chains. However, they were not prepared for *Shop, Save, and Share* graduates. Go to each store and buy their particular loss leaders (without Aunt Harriet), and you'll save BIG!

Lights, Camera, Action!

The Price Is Right!

Tips to Determining Value

What does grocery shopping have in common with a TV game show? First of all, if we were on television, we'd have to be clearheaded, on our toes, alert! That is, if we want to win the game. In shopping, it's the same way: We win at the store by paying attention to what we are doing and making sure that the price is right. Which (surprise, surprise) reminds me of another story.

We were living at George Air Force Base in the High Desert of Victorville, California, only a couple of hours from Los Angeles and Hollywood. It was the first time I'd ever lived on the West Coast. Months earlier several of my new California friends had taken the air force's Morale, Welfare, and Recreation (MWR) bus to the studios of *The Price Is Right.*

They excitedly filled me in on how they had been treated as members of the studio audience. First, they told me, everyone—all the audience members—had to endure a long wait, in a long line, for a long time. Then the producer interviewed each person and selected potential contestants. You didn't have to compete to be in the audience, that was a given. However, if you wanted to be a contestant, you had to stand out in the interview of the masses. The producer determined the contestants he felt would draw attention and add excitement on camera.

According to our friends who took the trip, the people chosen to be contestants had three characteristics: They were (1) outgoing, vivacious, talkative, and/or (2) did something unusual for a living, and/or (3) were part of a stereotypical group. The politically correct game show clusters were usually made up of the following mix: one senior-citizen male, one senior-citizen female, one person in uniform, one foreigner, two twenty-something or thirty-something males, and two twenty-something or thirty-something females.

I determined I would join the next busload to the show. Since the majority of the studio audience would be other homemakers in their twenties and thirties, I was in for some very tough competition. How could I stand out? Three shows were filmed each taping day. The studio audience for each show was limited to three hundred people. They picked nine contestants for each show from the audience members. The producer had to quickly interview *nine hundred people* each day they taped—to select twenty-seven contestants. What fun.

All *The Price Is Right* auditioners were asked one question and one question only: "What do you do for a living?" I had one chance to prove myself vivacious and outgoing. I couldn't answer, "I'm a homemaker." I knew the producer would yell, "NEXT!"

I stayed awake all night practicing my upcoming, two-second interview. When the big day arrived, we boarded the MWR bus to Burbank, checked in at the studio, and waited for hours.

Finally, it was our turn to audition for the contestant selections. First, we had to walk by the producer. As we watched the people in front of us being interviewed, I took a good look at the producer and his staff. He was a large man who sat in a director's chair and chomped on cigars. His assistant was blond (of course) and wore a black leather mini-skirt with *fishnet* panty hose. *Yep, this is Hollywood, all right,* I thought as I stared.

At last it was our turn. I was nervous but determined. *I want to get on that show,* I kept thinking. It had become a challenge to me and—what can I say?—I love a challenge.

The producer asked the pregnant lady next to me, "What do you do for a living?"

She smiled nervously, "I'm a mommy."

He chomped on his cigar and spat, "That's obvious! NEXT!"

The next person was one cool dude—you weren't going to see him sweat. He'd spent most of his time in line jiving with a friend.

The producer stared hard and asked, "What do you do for a living?"

The contestant wanna-be froze. He opened his mouth, but nothing came out. Then, slowly, he uttered his well-rehearsed speech: "Um...um...I'm an international...corporate attorney b-b-by...day... and...an exotic animal...um...hunter, no, trainer, b-b-by...uh...night."

The producer winked at his assistant, "Oh wow. Impressive. NEXT!"

It was my turn. When he asked the anticipated question, I immediately sprang into action. Reaching into my purse, I pulled out a mega grocery receipt, and exclaimed, *"THIS* is what I do." I swished my receipt in the air like a cheerleader. *I hope I'm animated enough.* "I show people how to save 50 to 85 percent on their food budget by using coupons and making sure that THE PRICE IS RIGHT." The producer just stared at me for a few seconds as I stood grinning like a cartoon statue of a crazed woman.

"That looks like a price list to me," he grunted.

Undaunted, I threw the receipt at him and replied, *"Here,* KEEP IT!" Then I smiled and said sweetly, "Something to remember me by."

About that time, I heard someone down the line mutter, "What a ham!"

As he glanced down at the receipt, the tough producer began to show signs of amazement. "Do you really save that much money?"

Suddenly, I felt fearless. I bubbled, "Yes, I do save that much money! And not only that, I LOVE Bob Barker. I LOVE *The Price Is Right.* And I would *REALLY LOVE* to be on the show!"

The assistant took a few notes. Then the producer nodded and yelled, "NEXT!"

I didn't know if I'd been selected—no one did—but I knew I had a pretty good chance.

As we filtered into the studio, we found our own seats in the auditorium. I sat in my chair and wondered, *Was I selected? I hope I'm one of "the chosen few." The suspense is going to kill me!*

After a while, the leather-clad blonde came onstage and looked into the studio audience, making even more notes. The woman sitting next to me was a veteran. She'd made seven attempts to get on the show. Authoritatively she informed me, "She's making notes for the studio cameras—indicating where the selected contestants are sitting."

The theme song played as the crowd, after hours of waiting, went wild. Announcements were made, the audience clapped, and the cameras rolled. When Bob Barker came onstage, the crowd went crazy. He was the great daytime hero of "TV-Game Showland." Four contestants were called. I wasn't one of them.

Halfway through the hour-long show, I was still sitting in my seat wondering. *Maybe I was a bit too hammy. I knew I should have worn red.* There were only two more chances to be a contestant. Things were looking bleak.

After the next commercial break, the announcer shouted, "Merry Christmas, *Ellie Kay*. You're the next contestant on *THE PRICE IS RIGHT!*"

I ran down the aisle, took my place at the podium, and smiled calmly. Gone was the ham. Instead, I concentrated on keeping my face slightly down—to get the best camera angle. I didn't want my double chin waving for attention on national television.

The item up for bid was a lovely wicker secretary and matching chair. "Oooo...aaaah!" crooned the audience.

Smiling into the camera, I made my bid. Miraculously—it held. I won and was invited to come onstage, where I was to play—get this—the grocery game. I'd seen *The Price Is Right* a few times and wasn't too familiar with the games. But I knew groceries.

In the $10,000 grocery game, there were several featured products with a target price of $2.25. For each product I chose under the target price, I got another zero added to my total. It started at $1.00 and I made enough correct choices to win $1,000.

Then Bob put his arm around me, smearing his makeup on my cheek, and asked the fateful question. "Now, Ellie, you've won $1,000. Do you want to keep it and end the game now? Or do you want to risk it all to try and win $10,000?" All I could see was zeros. I thought, *We sure need a new minivan.* With all the confidence I could muster I said, "I'll GO FOR IT, BOB!"

Bob pointed to a can of New Planters Snack Mix next to a bottle of Drano—I had to pick the one that was less than $2.25. The prices were incredibly inflated. I didn't know the value of the snack mix. The audience yelled, "PICK THE SNACKS! PICK THE SNACKS!" The pressure was intense. I reasoned the snack mix to be less expensive than the Drano, so I chose it.

The buzzer for the wrong answer was obnoxious. Especially when it meant I just lost $10,000 and that I'd also lost the $1,000 I'd won only moments before. The snack mix was $2.39, and the Drano was $1.77. To make matters worse, Bob Barker made a big deal over the fact that I lost.

They wouldn't let me go home because I had to spin the silly wheel to see if I'd make it to the Showcase Showdown. I got to spin *first*, since I'd *lost* earlier. The wheel was heavier than it looked, but I'd been pumping weights at the gym. I spun it as hard as I could and won a chance to play again. Things were looking up—I was going to the Showcase Showdown.

The bright lights were starting to get to me, and I figured the cameras were probably getting good shots of the real me—chins and all—by now. The first showcase had a silver punch bowl set and a video camera. Also included was an industrial cooking range with eight burners, two ovens, and a grill. My eyes grew wide. *That thing is bigger than the entire kitchen in our base house.* But the big prize in this first showcase was a twenty-foot Hi-Lo travel trailer. Our goal was to bid the closest to the actual retail price of the showcase—without going over. The other contestant, James, passed, and I bid $18,500. Everyone booed. I no longer cared; all I could think was *This show is ignorant.*

James's showcase had some weight sets and a speedboat. He bid $14,000 on his showcase. Bob cheerfully announced, "Jim, your showcase was valued at $13,990." Poor James missed the showcase by ten measly dollars. With the audience's booing still echoing in my ears, my less than optimistic attitude came out on camera.

I smiled stiffly and awaited Bob's announcement. "Ellie, do you remember what you bid?"

"No, Bob," I teased. "I don't remember what I bid."

"You bid $33,000!" he joked.

Bob gave one more parental chuckle. "Just kidding now, Ellie, you bid $18,500." He slowly opened the envelope. "The actual price of your showcase is $19,600. YOU WIN!"

What? My brain struggled to digest this news. *You mean, like, I won the entire showcase?*

Momentarily, I lost my composure. I squealed with delight, covering my face with my hands. Then I remembered the ever-present camera. Lowering my chin, I smiled gracefully into the wonderful world of television, thinking of my husband. "Hi, Beloved! Boy, am I having a great time on this *delightful* game show!"

On the way home, I was the MWR bus babe. My stardom continued into the next week as the local newspaper announced my win. To this day, my *Price Is Right* story impresses all kinds of people, from janitors to generals. I had worried about camera angles. My Beloved worried about the income taxes.

What is the point of this lengthy story? Well, if you use coupons faith-fully, provide for those in need, and happen to travel to Burbank, then you might get on *The Price Is Right.* God might bless you with winning the showcase. Finally, if you do win, you *will* have to pay taxes as earned income on the total amount of your winnings. Just ask my Beloved.

Okay, so I can't promise you a new travel trailer, cooking range, or video camera. But I can promise you delightful surprises as you honor God with the simple things—even couponing. I can also promise to give you some tips that will help you save a winning amount of money. If you are willing to be creative, to march—even occasionally—to a different beat—life will be more exciting.

Just think, if I hadn't brought my grocery receipt, if I had not stood out in the crowd as a Coupon Queen among queens—I'd have missed a fun, once-in-a-lifetime experience. Not to mention becoming the proud owner of a stove so big it could only fit in the living room.

It's made a lovely and unusual conversation piece.

Tips to Determining Value
How Do You Know If the Price Is Right?

Invest in a Credit-Card Size Calculator
This is a must for a half-wit, and even if you have all your wits about you, it will make those price determinations faster. I keep mine inside my coupon box for quick access, and you'll need it to help with some of the tips to follow.

Take Your Coupon Box to the Store
You should consider taking your coupon box with you to the store each time you shop. Many store sales are unadvertised. It's hard to take advantage of a sale and a (double) coupon without the coupon. You must have your coupon box in tow to determine if the price is right.

Check the Gimmicks
Just because there's a lovely yellow sale tag on the shelf does not

mean we'll buy it. In-store sales account for 50 percent of the total items on sale each week—the other sale products are in weekly or monthly sale circulars.

Evaluate each sales tag individually, as the reduction can be anywhere from 10 percent off the regular price to 75 percent off. I usually don't buy an item marked down by only a few pennies—I try to see past the "sale" gimmick and wait for a bigger discount.

Check the Coupon Value

Good couponing is *not* buying something simply because you have a coupon. Good couponing is buying a product with a coupon because it's a good value. To determine the price of each product, deduct the sales price, the coupon, and the double-coupon value (if applicable).

Here's one of my examples: Pritikin soup

Regular price	$1.89	*Never* pay full price
Sale Savings	- .70	Buying on sale saved 35%
Subtotal	$1.19	
Coupon	- .50	Saves an additional 25%
Double Coupon	- .50	Saves yet another 25%
Total Price Paid	**$0.19**	A total savings of 85% over retail

I'd say the price is right on the Pritikin soup.

Check the Smaller Sizes

A common misconception is that family-size or econo-size is cheaper. Actually, many of these items cost more per ounce than their smaller-sized counterparts. By using that inexpensive calculator, you can determine the unit price (per ounce, pound, count, etc.). Compare the prices of the various sizes. Some stores have the unit price on the shelf tag. Remember to deduct the value of the coupon.

With the coupon advantage, you can often get smaller-size items free—which is even cheaper than paying pennies for a larger size. This week I got the smallest count of Glad storage bags free with a double coupon, as well as the eight-ounce size of Kraft salad dressing. This is the time to stock up—at the right price!

Look for Overstocked, Bargain Bin, and Discontinued Items

We're not talking about buying canned goods with mold growing out of the dents. Sometimes stores have discontinued or overstocked products in a special section on the shelves, or they might be in a grocery cart at the back of the store—ask the store manager. Because of store regulations, many foods that are still wholesome are price reduced when they approach their expiration dates.

Many of these price-reduced items can be wonderful bargains—and you can use your coupons on them as well! Ask the butcher and produce managers what's about to expire and offer to take it off their hands at a reduced price.

Make Bulk-Buying the Exception Rather Than the Rule

The *Shop, Save, and Share* system is a different way of viewing grocery shopping. Most of the items I buy are price reduced and have a double coupon. Therefore, I've paid the lowest price possible on these items—less than shopping at a warehouse club.

Paper towels were on sale last week for 59¢ per roll. I had a 20¢ coupon, doubled—so with four coupons, I got each roll for only 19¢. The warehouse club had a twelve-pack of the same paper towels for $5.88, or 49¢ a roll. Which is the better bargain?

There are a few grocery products I'll buy at a warehouse club—yeast, for instance—but very few. I do much better at a regular grocery store.

Buy in Season

Most produce items purchased in season are at least worthy of the saying *Buy Now, Freeze Later.* Buy them *on sale* in season and save even more. Freezing directions are printed on most freezer bags; it's usually a matter of blanching the produce with boiling water, then freezing them.

Here's an easy seasonal buying guide:

Vegetable	Peak Season
Artichokes	March–May
Asparagus	April–May
Beets	June–October
Broccoli	October–April
Brussels sprouts	October–February
Cauliflower	October
Corn	May–September
Okra	June–August
Peas	May–September
Sweet potatoes	September–December
Tomatoes	May–August

Fruit	Peak Season
Apples	September–March
Apricots	June–July
Blueberries	June–July
Cantaloupe	June–August
Cherries	June–July
Cranberries	September–December
Figs	June–October
Grapefruit	October–May
Peaches	July–August
Pears	July–October
Plums	May–September
Raspberries	July
Strawberries	April–June
Watermelon	June–August

Write in the Price of "Free" Items

Periodically, manufacturers release coupons for free items to get you to try their new product. These also include buy one/get one free coupons. There is usually a place provided on the coupon to write in the price. For example, when Reese's introduced the Cookie Crunch Peanut Butter Cup with a free coupon, I saved all the coupons I could locate from our community swapbox (more about this swapbox in chapter 3) and got thirty-five free candy bars. (I was an instant hero to my munchkins.)

I wrote the price on each coupon and saved the checker time and effort. It is frustrating for checkers to have to look over an entire mega-receipt to locate the price of one small item, so do part of the checker's work for them. Which brings me to our final tip.

Make Friends With Your Local Checkers

I try to help my local checkers in every way possible, and to abide by the store's written and unwritten rules. One of the unwritten rules at our local grocer's is to place all your groceries on the conveyor belt and then place the appropriate coupon on top of each item. This takes a little more time, but if it helps them, cooperation can help you in the long run. I also try to make a game out of the transaction experience. Who can guess my coupon savings—the checker or me?

Since most checkers require a break after one of my grueling check-outs, I try not to tax anyone's strength two weeks in a row. Ed is one of my favorite checkers who enjoys my half-witted games—at least that's what he tells me. When I went through another checker's line last week, he saw me and called out. "Hey, are you saving a lot of money today, Mrs. Kay?"

I laid a Cheerios coupon on top of the box of cereal. "Yes, Ed. I'm going to save over one hundred dollars this week."

He appeared a little hurt as he looked down at his feet for a moment. "Well, why didn't you come through my line today?"

I stopped loading groceries and looked at him, "Why, Ed, it's because you had to endure my check-out marathon last week. I thought I'd give you a break."

He ran his hands through his hair. "Aw, shucks, Mrs. Kay! I like getting you. I like to see how much money you save."

See! Not *all* checkers scream and run for the break room when the Coupon Queen arrives.

Where Do
You Find Those
Critters?

Tips to Locating Coupons

A s a half-witted mother of five, married to a military man, I've had to manage lots of events on my own. The birth of our fourth child, for example. Bob was the aide-de-camp to a three-star general. What does such a prestigious aide do? He serves coffee and works fifteen- to eighteen-hour days. When I called Bob to announce junior's imminent arrival, he was at the general's house working a reception for the secretary of the air force. Later, Bob told me he dropped his coffee and spilled his cellular phone. Or was it the other way around? Anyway, he panicked—in the same way he's reacted to our other children's births. I told my husband, "You don't need to leave your important reception until the last minute. After all, if the secretary's coffee isn't fresh, it might mean the beginning of another cold war."

My Beloved told the general about the BIG event, and since the general's house was only five minutes away from our house, the two of them called me every ten minutes for updates. I know, you civilians might be appalled that Bob didn't come home immediately. If you are, you don't understand the military. I was a real trooper—for a while. As the contractions got harder, I became less understanding.

When they were two minutes apart, I called Bob again. "I've decided NOW would be a good time for you to get your coffee-pounding body home and take me to the hospital." The labor was fast and hard and lasted only an hour and a half. In the labor and delivery room, Bob turned on the TV "to keep you distracted during the rough labor." Yeah, right. As any woman knows, it takes more than television to distract her from what feels like an elephant stepping on her midsection.

The show happened to be a favorite in the Kay household. There were two problems with this: (1) Bob goes into the twilight zone when he turns on a television, and (2) I felt he needed to coach me, not distract himself with what was supposed to be distracting me!

Thankfully, my friend Patti arrived just in time to rub my back. Despite her best efforts, I still needed my *Be-lov-ed* (syllable emphasis indicates level of frustration) in my face to help me breathe.

Despite my TV-impaired coach, despite the fact my labor was transitioning from bad to worse, and despite the all-natural-no-drugs-at-all-why-in-the-world-am-I-doing-it-this-way-childbirth method, I managed to scream, "WHERE IS JESUS? WHERE IS HE?" That got *almost* everyone's attention in the room.

"He's right here, Ellie," soothed Patti.

Bob absently and fondly patted the lampshade. "Mega dittos."

I looked wildly into Patti's eyes. "WELL, I KNOW HE SAYS HE'S ALWAYS WITH US, BUT I DON'T SEE HIM ANYWHERE! I THINK I NEED SOME DRUGS AFTER ALL!"

An experienced nurse, Patti took my face firmly between her hands and said, "Now, Ellie, settle down. You know you can do this—you've done it before. It's almost over."

Bob agreed, "That's right, Beloved, soon we'll see our newest little Kay. But if you could just hold off ten more minutes, I'd appreciate it. There's a segment coming up on the balanced budget."

Even though I couldn't talk, my mind was working well enough to know that a certain fighter pilot would be finished if he didn't turn off that blasted show!

Jonathan David entered the world ten minutes later, just as the show ended—and just in time to get Bob's attention.

What does this tender story have to do with coupons? Good question. The point I want to make is that you don't have to organize these coupons alone. Your coach won't be a distracted dittohead, and the process isn't nearly as painful as childbirth. In fact, it can be lots of fun. This system is so organized there's nothing left to speculation, even though some of the steps may be different from what you're used to. The end result will be a beautifully organized baby of a shopping system you can take to the bank. (Or at least to the store.)

Tips to Locating Coupons

The Sunday Newspaper

Freestanding inserts (FSIs) are found in the center section of the newspaper. They're printed on glossy paper and regularly distributed by manufacturers. A good paper will have two to three packets of FSIs.

If you live in a small town, the local paper may not carry coupons. Call the newspaper office of the nearest city and ask about home delivery. If they mail the paper, make sure they'll include coupons. Most newspapers allow a Sunday-only subscription. I get *three* Sunday-only newspaper subscriptions. This small investment yields a great return.

Some cities have newsstands or convenience stores that display papers before purchase. It is better to get papers at a store than at a self-service newspaper machine. Many newspaper distributors don't bother to include coupons in papers placed in machines. Unfortunately, people tend to steal coupons out of machine papers. Whereas, in a store, you can check each paper for coupons before you buy them.

"Hi, Mom!"—Friends and Family

Oftentimes manufacturers will test a specified market area in a certain part of the country. Before these coupons or products are released nationwide, they are distributed in the market area and sales are evaluated. Consequently, friends in another state *may* have access to coupons that aren't available to you. Also, different parts of the country may release different values on the same coupon. For example, in New York our stores double coupons up to $1.00. Most of the Kellogg's coupons are for $1.00 off *two*. My friend in New Mexico, Farrell Morton, sends me the same Kellogg's coupons for 75¢ off *one*. They only double up to 50¢ in her part of the world. Instead of getting 50¢ off a box of cereal (with my local coupon), I got $1.50 off at the double coupon store with Farrell's coupon.

Ask friends and family to save and mail you the coupons they do not use. If you have to send them postage money for their efforts, it's still worth it. Tell your co-workers, neighbors, and church friends you are collecting coupons. Most people are happy to give away coupons so they'll be used rather than thrown away. I cringe at the thought of people *throwing away* coupons.

Mailing Lists/Clipless Store Coupons

Ask the local grocers if they have a store mailing list or special store card. Sometimes these cards are for check-cashing privileges, and other times they are for the store's clipless coupon card. A clipless coupon gives the customer the advantage of store sales and cents off hundreds of products on a weekly basis. Once you're on a store's mailing list, you are eligible to receive store promotions by mail—including sale advertisements and coupons. These should not be confused with national coupon clubs.

Some surveys state that as many as 85 percent of all coupon clubs are illegal. Usually, the customer picks the coupons he wants and pays a fee. The "club" sends manufacturer's coupons without the manufacturer's consent. Even if you found a legal club, the same $30 could be spent on a couple of dozen Sunday newspapers (with FSIs) for a better value.

Product Packages/Instant Rebates

As coupon use increases, you may develop a "coupon radar" to detect unclaimed coupons. A coupon radar hones in on product packages with coupons on them. Coupon offers are oftentimes advertised on the product, e.g., "$3 in coupons inside!" These may be located on the package itself and could be a challenge to find. Check the box or carton carefully before you throw it away. There may also be loose coupons inside the package. These are usually located in between the plastic paper and the product box. These coupons tend to be lower in value than FSI coupons, but they usually have longer expiration dates.

Other products have instant rebates or coupons *attached to the outside* of the product that should be removed and redeemed immediately at the check-out. These are usually on top of the product and readily visible. Remember to check each item as you put it in your cart for manufacturer's coupons attached to the product. Most of the time, these coupons are good only at the time of purchase—so use it or lose it!

Magazines

Your radar should beep loudly around magazines that have coupons in them. In terms of investment, it's not wise to buy a magazine subscription exclusively for the purpose of acquiring coupons. There's not a good financial return based on a subscription cost investment. Magazine manufacturer's coupons tend to be lower in value with longer expiration dates. However, it is wise to examine your existing subscriptions for those valuable coupons.

Manufacturer Direct

In the competitive product merchandising market, companies are realizing the value of customer service and satisfaction. Many of today's products have toll-free numbers listed directly on their labels. Sometimes these numbers are to report product defects, but you don't know until you call. If you do have a defective product, call the number and you should receive a coupon for another like item. You may have to send in the defective product; the company will let you know.

Even if you don't have a problem, call these phone numbers and let them know what you think of their product—especially if you like it! Ask them if they have any coupons they can mail to you. Almost all of the companies will send you free recipes. Not every phone call will be profitable, but those that are will make your time investment prove valuable. While you have them on the phone, ask for their website or email address. Which brings us to our next resource.

Cyberspace—The Unexplored Frontier

Many manufacturers have their own websites on the super information highway. With their address, as obtained in our last tip, you can surf the net to download coupons or have them mail the coupons, recipes, and other offers to your home. If you are not on the web, try your local library. You can use their computer with your website addresses in hand, and the librarian will help you find these companies. Many manufacturers are located by typing www. their name in lowercase letters, followed by .com. For example, www.colgate.com.

There is also a growing number of websites containing coupons that you can print out and use at your local store. One site (www.valuepage.com, featured in the June 18, 1998, *Wall Street Journal*) allows you to pick a participating grocery store in your zip code to see what their coupon specials include. The value of the coupons averages about $35 per week. Other valuable sites that focus on general products include www.freeshop.com, www.coolsavings.com, www.hotcoupons.com, and www.supermarkets.com.

Electronic Coupons

Many grocery stores now have an electronic coupon system. These coupons are dispensed by machines, directly on aisle shelves, throughout the store. In addition, Check-out coupons are issued at the check-out, and are a good value on future purchases. We'll define and differentiate between these coupons in the next chapter.

Direct Marketing

Do you know the surveys in newspapers and magazines that promise free samples and coupons if you fill out their survey? Well, they work! You may get some junk mail to throw in the recycling bin, but you'll also get on a direct mailing list for future coupons. Other direct marketing packets that come in the mail are the Carol Wright advertising envelopes. If you sift through the disposable "offers" you'll run across some good manufacturer's coupons.

Watch those packets of junk mail for some real treasures. I routinely get my film developed by a mail-in photo lab. The film envelopes in the junk mail services offer lower prices than the film envelopes mailed to me by the company itself. I save almost $2.00 a roll!

Bonus Tip: The Coupon Swapbox

A local coupon swapbox is very easy to use and organize. Furthermore, it is free. Any group can establish a swapbox. All you need is some people with the common goal of swapping coupons. I've seen swapboxes located in churches, outside grocery stores, in community service buildings, in play groups, homeschool groups, and in the workplace.

There are many methods of trading coupons, ranging from a big box of completely unorganized coupons for people to rummage through (highly ineffective), to coupons arranged in categories (which requires a tremendous amount of work to maintain). I came across a simple, yet effective system developed in our church when we were stationed in Columbus, Mississippi. My friend Madeline introduced me to it.

This non-high-tech method is known as the "baggie system" because it uses ordinary sandwich bags—the zipping variety work best. When someone has fifty or more coupons they want to contribute, they put them in a plastic bag. Then they write their name on the top line of a plain index card, place it in the bag, and put the bag in the swapbox. The swapbox itself is just a shoebox-size plastic box with a lid. A central location is established for the organization's swapbox.

Next, a person picks a bag someone else contributed and looks through the coupons in that bag. They remove the coupons they need and put them aside. Then they sign their name under the previous name on the index card and replace the bag in the swapbox. DO NOT PUT NEW COUPONS IN EXISTING BAGS. Instead, start a new bag with coupons you are contributing. If your name is already on an index card, you don't need to look through that particular bag of coupons.

At the end of each month, a coupon coordinator reviews the bags and removes expired coupons. This keeps the system up-to-date. It is efficient because it only takes a few minutes to look through a bag, and it is effective because many people can participate to whatever extent they choose, and at the same time.

When I establish a new swapbox, I print out the following directions and place them on top of the coupon box with thick, clear, heavy-duty tape or clear contact paper. Feel free to copy the directions provided on the next page for your organization's swapbox.

Remember, you'll need a coupon coordinator to go through the bags each month and pull out expired coupons. Technique: When I've pulled the expired coupons from the previous month, I write that month followed by an "ED" for expiration date. That notation on the name card lets me know I've pulled all the expired coupons from that bag. For example, in the month of November, I'll pull all of October's expired coupons and write "October ED" on the name card.

The coordinator should contact a local military organization to donate the expired coupons. Expired coupons are good up to six months past the expiration date in overseas military commissaries. Oftentimes, coupons mailed from the States are the only coupons these families receive. There are blanks provided on the instructions for the coordinator's name and phone number. Happy swapping!

Coupon Swapbox Instructions

1. Coupons are in zipping plastic bags and contain a name card in the front of each bag. A name card is an index card-size piece of paper with names signed on it.
2. Please take a bag and remove the coupons you want from that bag. Sign your name on the name card. DO NOT ADD NEW COUPONS TO AN EXISTING BAG.
3. Put the coupons you're donating in a new bag with your name signed on a new name card. Place the new bag in the swapbox.
4. In the future, only pick those bags without your name on the name card. (You've already gone through the coupons in the bags with your name on them.)
5. Place all your expired coupons in the bag marked "EXPIRED COUPONS." We will send these to military families overseas.
6. Have fun! If you have any questions, please call the coupon coordinator,_____at_____.

"Real" Men Fly Jets, but Can They Organize Coupons?

Tips to Defining Coupons

Fighter pilots are a rare breed. They thrive on the kind of adventure that would make sane people invest in bladder control products. I know if I were to fly 500 knots at 100 feet off the ground, I'd want a supply of Attends tucked in my flight bag. It wouldn't be so bad because I have a $2.00 coupon, and, of course, I'd buy them on sale—but that's beside the point. As I was saying, pilots are a little different. They abide by their own creed, use their own acronyms, and play their own little games—like Crud.

The game of Crud is an exclusive fighter-pilot-created pool table game. There are a lot of silly rules to Crud. Basically the game is played on an extra long pool table using a white ball and a striped ball. The object is to hit your opponent's ball with the white ball in such a way that they lose a "life." After three lives, you're out of the game. The team with the last living player wins. Of course, you can't play your ball from anywhere but the ends of the table, you must have a foot on the floor at the time you release the ball, and you can't play out of turn. If you make any of these infractions—it's your life! Understand? I knew you would. Now we can play!

I like playing Crud, and I'm pretty good at it too. My long arms and legs make me the ideal player—for a girl.

We had many functions to attend at the Academy while Bob was a commander of a squadron of cadets. There were promotion ceremonies, football games, intramural sports games, changes of command, cadet balls, dinners, receptions—you get the idea? Every now and then, when we were in the Officer's Club for a function, we'd try to play a couple of games before going back home to the herd. It helped break the monotony known in the military as "mandatory fun."

One night we put aside our Diet Cokes and recruited people for a game of Crud. There were a few "heavy" pilots there (meaning guys who flew BIG airplanes) who had never played. So we taught them and some of the medical officers the finer points of a fun sport. We were having a great time. That is, until we heard a loud growl in the hallway. Moose had arrived.

Moose got his name from his glory days at the Academy as a starting center on the football team. He lived up to his nickname in every way—especially his call sign when he flew the F-15. Now, there's something you should know about these fighter types. Every one of them thinks he's the "World's Best Fighter Pilot." He also believes his particular jet is the best weapon system in the world. Moose was no exception. The F-15 is one of the newer airplanes on the block. It was the snazziest airplane in the air force—just ask him, he'd tell you.

So Moose let us know he wanted to play. Who was going to tell the giant man with antlers to go home? Moose ruled the game through brute force and sheer intimidation. When there was a call he didn't like, he'd stand up to his full height, suck air deep into his barrel chest, and bellow his displeasure.

As I stood on the sidelines, awaiting my turn, I watched Moose argue yet another referee decision. He was acting like an overgrown schoolboy, and his bellyaching was slowing down the game. No one would do anything about it. I started to stew. I thought, *We were having a lot of fun before he showed up*. I was getting angry.

As I saw Moose yell at a pilot half his size, another thought occurred to me. *I'm paying a baby-sitter six dollars an hour! For what? This kind of nonsense? Is he going to get away with this? Am I going to stand here and take it?*

By now, I wasn't just *kind* of angry, I was *way* angry. No one cheats a half-witted mother out of her special night on the town with her Beloved. *No one robs me of a bargain! Everyone else might be intimidated, but I'm not. I've got ways of dealing with a toddler's temper tantrums!*

I saw a waiter nearby. To gather my courage, I ordered a milk—straight up, no chocolate. When my drink arrived, I downed it in one, long gulp. Braced by the extra calcium, I slowly crossed the room to Moose. He stood beside the Crud table, his fists clenched, yelling at the referee.

I tapped him on the shoulder and he turned around to face me. To be precise, we were face to belly button. I grabbed a nearby chair and stood on it, giving me a better vantage point. I had him right where I wanted him—eyeball to eyeball.

He was a little surprised—and amused. "Ah, it's Miss Ellie," he smirked.

He looked around the room, which had become very quiet, and cleared his throat. "Don't you think it's about time you went home to tuck in those little ones?"

That does it, Buster! I thought. Then, glaring into his cold blue eyes, I said, "No, Moose. It's not time for me to go home."

There was an audible intake of breath by those standing nearby. A small, astonished crowd had gathered to watch the woman with a milk mustache take on Goliath.

Just about that time, Bob reentered the room. He'd left to make a phone call—checking on the baby-sitter. He took one look at the quiet room and took another look at me on the chair. He gave me an imploring, nonverbal expression that said, "I can't believe you are doing this! Please come down from there—*please?*"

I was unmoved. I had some business to settle, and I was on a roll.

Moose was shocked into silence.

My eyes narrowed as only an angry mother's can. It was Moose's turn to be lambasted. "We were having fun before you came. All you've done is refuse to take turns, argue with the boys, and act ugly to the referee."

I grabbed him by the collar of his flight suit, "You'd better stop your tantrums *and* your bellyaching or you'll just have to GO HOME!"

By now, the entire club was so silent you could hear a cue ball drop. Red-faced, Bob was so upset he was drinking my milk. The roomful of people watched in amazement. Was this the same woman who baked snickerdoodles for the entire senior class of cadets? Wasn't this the mild-mannered woman who taught coupon seminars?

Moose didn't know what to do—it had been so long since someone had actually challenged him. He looked at the rabid, half-witted mama standing before him. He knew his options.

He glanced around the room. There was only one thing to do.

He glanced down at his feet. "Aw, shucks! I'm sorry, Miss Ellie. Don't make me go home right now." He started to wring his hands. "I'll act better—I promise!"

I patted the big lug on the head. "It's all right, Michael, I forgive you."

The room exhaled in unison and the game continued—with "Be nice" as the new rule to the game of Crud.

After the match was over, Bob approached Moose and gave him a sympathetic smile. My husband lowered his voice so as not to be overheard by the others, "Better to have a bandit on your tail at six o'clock and lose vector control than to meet a half-wit robbed of her fun night out."

Fighter pilots aren't so hard to understand—you just have to know how to handle them.

Wise shoppers have a lot in common with fighter pilots. We're both professionals. We follow rules in the shopping game others may think silly—but we'll win the price war. Pilots have their own lingo: check six, lead turn, procedure, and technique—to name a few. In the same way, Coupon Queens have their own "language." This chapter discusses different kinds of coupon definitions in combat grocery shopping. First we'll need to define a couple of flying terms that apply to professional grocery shoppers.

I'd like to make one final point about advanced couponers—we don't back down from a challenge. After all, most of us have faced down a toddler or two in need of a nap.

Tips to Defining Coupons

Procedures Versus Techniques

When Bob was an instructor pilot, he taught young men and women to fly fighter aircraft. He frequently used two terms: procedure and technique.

A *procedure* is a routine followed by the book. Understanding a procedure doesn't matter. It simply must be observed in order for the system to be effective. In couponing, certain procedures are followed because they're part of the overall system. The system works efficiently when these procedures are observed—whether you initially understand them or not.

On the other hand, a *technique* is not written in stone. It is a method that is flexible. Basically, it's whatever works best for you. Techniques fit the saying "Blessed are the flexible, for they shall not be broken." In couponing, technique means you find certain things work best for you. The same techniques may or may not work for others. For example, I choose to highlight the expiration dates on my coupons *before* I cut them, rather than *after*. I think this is more efficient and faster. Others may want to highlight *after* they've cut out their coupons. Therein lies the difference between a technique and a procedure.

Clip Every Coupon—Procedure

In organizing coupons, it is a *procedure* to clip every coupon. You will not *use* every coupon, but it's important to clip every one. The coupons you don't use are donated to a swapbox. Or give them away. I give all my dog food coupons to friends with dogs. With five kids, who needs a dog?

There are reasons people tend to eliminate a variety of coupons. For example, some people may not clip coupons for highly sugared cereals and/or salty processed mixes because they don't use them for health reasons. Whether *you* use the item or not, it's important to clip the coupon. On the other hand, another person won't clip coupons for Colgate toothpaste because their mama made them use Colgate five times a day for eighteen years. They're traumatized by that brand of toothpaste. Or they won't buy Aquafresh for their children because their kids don't like the color. Get the idea?

The reason to clip and file coupons on these items is—drum roll, please. You never know when an item will be free with that coupon. If you have the right coupon, you can purchase some items for a few pennies. Even if you don't use Colgate, you could get it free and give it to someone else—the local homeless shelter, a crisis pregnancy shelter, or a food pantry. You could even get a tax deduction for donated food. The bottom line is, you could provide for someone in need.

Clip Every Coupon—Technique

Since every rule (or procedure) has an exception, I don't clip absolutely *every* coupon. I don't clip alcohol or cigarette coupons. I believe these items don't meet people's health "needs." So in all good conscience, I can't pass along coupons that may undermine someone's well-being.

To illustrate my point, let's paint a hypothetical picture. What if I *did* clip these coupons and get some of these items free?

Just imagine, which isn't too hard for me, that I've had one of those days when the kids draw clown faces on the baby—with *permanent* marker. A day when they drink all the milk and pretend they're Bill Nye, the Science Guy. Then they put the bottle in a 350° oven to see what will happen.

Even though I do not smoke or drink, I could be tempted. Picture me after a no good, very bad day, sitting at the kitchen table with a wine cooler, puffing away on a slender cigarette. Bob comes home and stares at me with his mouth open. Could it be justified with "But, Beloved—" puff, puff, gulp, "—I had to get them, they were FREE!"? Me thinketh not. My technique is: I don't clip every coupon.

I have found diapers for 98¢ a bag, sugared cereals free, and highly salted, processed boxes of noodles for pennies, and I give them away. I get these products when they are on sale when I have a manufacturer's coupon and/or I have a store coupon. Which brings us to our next section. "What is a store coupon?"

Advanced Couponing—The Master's Course

Just as rules change in life, so coupon rules change from state to state, city to city, store to store, and sometimes—checker to checker. Some of these rules are subject to change without warning.

I must add a note at this time. The definitions of coupon terms in this section are extremely technical. They may even sound like Greek to those new to coupon shopping. Much of the following material is for students in the graduate school of coupon shopping. I encourage the novice to read and reread this section as they begin to use coupons at the store.

You don't have to master the material in order to save money and give away groceries. However, I'm including this additional material for those who desire a professional challenge.

There are several types of coupons available in grocery stores in modern America. There are also new coupon concepts introduced regularly. The primary coupons are: manufacturer's coupons, store coupons, competitor's coupons, electronic coupons, and check-out coupons.

Manufacturer's Coupon—The Basic Black Dress

A manufacturer's coupon is the basic black dress of the coupon set. It is the most common coupon. Sometimes, it can be combined with other offers. A manufacturer's coupon is issued and reimbursed by the company that makes the product. The front of a manufacturer's coupon will always have a mailing address for the corporation of issue. A manufacturer's coupon may be for *cents off* a product, a particular *price* on a product, or a *free* product (see Figure 1-A on page 52).

Some manufacturers participate in special promotions with a particular store chain. They allow the store to reproduce their coupon in the store's sale material. This particular kind of manufacturer's coupon adds the name of the store on the coupon itself (see Figure 1-B). This particular coupon should not be confused with a store coupon.

Store Coupons

A store coupon (see Figure 1-C) is issued by a grocery, drug, or discount store and may be redeemed only at the store of issue. Some coupons *appear* to be store coupons because they have the store name printed on the in-ad coupon. Actually, they are *manufacturer's* coupons that can be redeemed only at that particular store (see Figure 1-B). The best way to identify a store coupon is to read the fine print. If a coupon has a store name but a manufacturer's address on it for redemption purposes, then it is a *manufacturer's* coupon. If it has the *store* name *and address* on it, or *no address*, then it is a *store* coupon.

When in doubt, ask the checker or the store manager whether the coupon in question is a store coupon or a manufacturer's coupon. Some checkers are not familiar with the technical aspect of coupons, so you might have to go directly to a front end store manager. It is a matter of being familiar enough with your material.

The Feds—It's All About Funding

The federal government regulates the coupon industry. That's why coupon fraud is a federal offense. I heard a story about the coupon crime queen, "Coupon Connie." It would be safe to say she got a little carried away and ended up facing some time in jail.

Back to store coupons for a moment. The reason a store coupon will not have a manufacturer's address anywhere on the coupon (see Figure 1-C) is because a store coupon is funded by money from the store and *not* the manufacturer. The sources of reimbursement are different.

Consequently, it is *usually* acceptable to combine two different sources of reimbursement together. If the store allows it (and most stores will), it is all right to use two coupons (a store coupon and a manufacturer's coupon) on one product.

I'll repeat this radical idea. When the *store* issues the coupon (a true store coupon), it can usually be used in conjunction with a manufacturer's coupon. The exception to this rule is if the coupon specifically states that the store coupon *cannot* be used in conjunction with a manufacturer's coupon. Or if the grocery store advertises a policy *against* the use of these coupons in conjunction. A store coupon is funded by the marketing department of the store. The manufacturer's coupon is funded by the manufacturer. Different bank accounts—different sources of funding.

Confused in Connecticut? Hopeless in Hampford? Don't worry, you can always come back to this chapter when you graduate with a degree in couponing. This is the Master's stuff, and you don't have to learn it all in one sitting! These definitions will still be here when you come back. Still confused? Then don't read on.

Competitor's Coupons

Store coupons are closely related to competitor's coupons. A competitor's coupon comes into the equation only at stores that advertise: *We honor all competitor's coupons.* If none of your local stores offers this great benefit, then don't worry about this section.

If a store honors all competitor's coupons, it does not mean they will honor other store's advertised *prices*, only their advertised *coupons*. Unless, of course, they advertise: *We'll match any competitor's price.* This does mean that the store will accept store coupons (see Figure 1-C), and in-ad manufacturer's coupons (see Figure 1-B) from *other* stores. When a *store coupon* is redeemed at a different store, it becomes a *competitor's coupon*.

When an in-ad manufacturer's coupon is used at a different store, it is technically a competitor's coupon. The reason it is a competitor's coupon and not a manufacturer's coupon lies in the bank account. For example, if Albertson's issued an in-ad manufacturer's coupon: *Save $2 with coupon on ONE, any CLAIROL hair color.* It also stipulates: *Good only at Albertson's.* This indicates that Albertson's marketing department and Clairol's marketing department entered into an agreement:

Albertson's is authorized to print Clairol's coupons in their sales circular.

Another store, such as Smith's, does not share Albertson's agreement with Clairol on the specific in-ad manufacturer's coupon. Therefore, if a customer redeemed the Albertson's coupon at Smith's (because it honors competitor's coupons), Clairol is not legally bound to reimburse Smith's. The agreement was for Albertson's. Smith's must enter into their own agreement with Clairol. They must print their own in-ad manufacturer's coupon in order for Clairol to be legally bound to reimburse that coupon.

Therefore, the Albertson's coupon is a competitor's coupon when redeemed at Smith's. *Usually*, it may be used in conjunction with a regular manufacturer's coupon—if Smith's does not have a policy against the use of competitor's coupons in conjunction with manufacturer's coupons. If a store has a policy against the combination of these coupons, then they may not be redeemed together on one item.

One time I shopped at Smith's grocery store when they advertised: *We honor competitor's coupons.* I took an *Albertson's* $2.00 off diapers coupon to Smith's for $2.00 off the store brand diapers. I also had a manufacturer's coupon for "Buy one/get one free" on the same diapers. The diapers were on sale for $3.99 a bag. The result borderlines on the miraculous!

Here's what happened:

Regular price of two bags of diapers $5.99 each	$11.98
Two bags of diapers on sale @$3.99 each (save 33%)	-$ 4.00
Sale price on two bags	$ 7.98
Subtract manufacturer's coupon (Buy one/get one free)	-$ 3.99
Subtract competitor's coupon	-$ 2.00
Total price for two bags of diapers	**$ 1.99**

And now for something simple!

Electronic Coupons

The electronic coupon (see Figure 2-B) is dispensed by a machine on the aisle shelves of the grocery store. The manufacturer or vendor enters into an agreement with a grocery chain to place their dispenser machines in the store for a specified amount of time. Most of these coupons are not subject to doubling as they read *coupon may not be doubled.* Unless the store has a policy for doubling these coupons as well, as our local store does.

Check-out Coupons—A Great Bonus at the Check-out!

Another kind of coupon is a check-out coupon (see Figure 2-A). It is issued at the check-out after your purchases are scanned into the register. The store computer tracks the products you buy and a printer prints the appropriate coupon. These coupons are usually manufacturer's coupons for cents off a particular product. They can also be "cash off" the next shopping trip and free products as well.

The cents-off coupons are used as any manufacturer's coupon. They are usually subject to doubling in double coupon stores. The cash-off coupons may be used (all at once) on the next trip to the store. For example, if I earned five "$1.00 off your next shopping trip" coupons, I could redeem all of these coupons on my next trip—and receive $5.00 off the total bill!

If a store offers check-out coupons, there is usually a sign under the product in the aisle stating the offer (see Figure 2-C.) The $1.00-off coupon should print electronically at the check-out. If it's advertised and does not print, call it to the manager's attention immediately to get the coupon equivalent.

The values offered on these coupons can help determine your purchases. For example, I bought a General Foods International Coffee Sample Pack at $2.09 per box. I had a 50¢-off manufacturer's coupon doubled and a 50¢-off competitor's coupon given at face value. Face value means you only get the amount of the coupon and you do not get a double bonus.

Here's how it looks:

General Foods Sample Pack	$2.09
Manufacturer's coupon	- .50
Store's double coupon offer	- .50
Competitor's coupon (face value)	- .50
Total	**$0.59**

Now the Coupon Queen may believe that 59¢ is too much to pay for coffee. However, the sign beneath the product indicated *Buy two, get $1.00 off your next shopping purchase.* Because $1.00 divided by two is an additional 50¢ off, in the long run (two shopping trips) I only paid 9¢ for that coffee!

Bonus Tip: It's a Contract!

Coupons, by design, are like contracts. Since they're federally regulated, they *must* use precise language. Consequently, the coupon must be specific in its limitations, or no limitations may be imposed on the consumer. For example, one coupon I had read: *40¢ off any Tampax package (except the four-pack size)*. There were *two*-pack trial sizes of this product in the store for 69¢. I used my coupon (which was doubled up to the value of the item) and got ten boxes free, because the coupon, or contract, read: "Not good on four-pack size." It did not specifically state, "Not good on four-pack size *or smaller*." Nor did it state, "Not good on two-pack size." It's to your advantage to read the fine print.

Grocers receive reimbursement from manufacturers for their costs in processing coupons. Many "contract out" these redemptions to professionals. As a result, stores *do not* lose money on coupons. As a matter of fact, they can *make* money on a high volume of processed coupons. One store manager with eighteen years experience, told me:

"It's hard to believe, Mrs. Kay, that we don't lose money on even someone like you.

"You would think that when a person only pays $35 for $150 worth of groceries, we would lose money. But the manufacturers reimburse us for their coupons and the store's marketing department reimburses us for double coupons and competitor's coupons. So coupons are just like cash to us. I *will* say that taking $115 in cash is a lot easier than taking $115 in coupons. Still, that's our job." (Boyd Moffitt, interview, January 1997).

Master's Level Bonus Tip

Remember to read the fine print on the coupon and abide by its stipulations. As we saw earlier, these rules can be in your favor. For example, a store is running a mega-sale on a 5 lb. bag of sugar for 99¢ with the store coupon. If the coupon contract states, "Limit one coupon per item," then collect several copies of the sale circular, buy several bags of sugar, and redeem them all at the same time. This saves the trouble of several trips to the store for the mega-special.

However, if the store coupon reads, "Limit one coupon per item and one coupon per customer," then you can only redeem one coupon at a time. Just remember—every trip to the store makes you a new customer. Children are customers, too, and it's a great opportunity to teach them. If the store coupon reads, "Limit one coupon per *family*," then your children must be claimed as part of your family. Even when Jonathan's licking the metal rail at the check-out and Bethany's doing her Ethel Merman imitation for the bored people in line—I still have to claim them.

Figure: 1-A

Figure: 1-B

Figure: 1-C

Figure: 2-A

Figure: 2-B

Figure: 2-C

How to Stuff
Five Children Into
Two Bedrooms —
And More Family Fun

Tips to Family Fun

We have chosen to live in military housing in all of our assignments. One advantage to life on base is the '50s kind of lifestyle in the neighborhoods. Folks still share an orange over the fence while watering their lawns. I borrow a cup of sugar from my neighbor. Leisurely walks and shoot-the-breeze talks are a regular part of summer pastimes. We let our children ride their bikes on the street and play at the playground with few worries for their safety. I feel secure when Bob goes on extended military business trips. It's a friendly, supportive environment.

Before you go to your local recruiter to join the air force, though, there is one primary disadvantage to military housing: dwelling size. When we arrived at our assignment at Holloman AFB in Alamogordo, New Mexico, we had a problem. My lieutenant colonel husband with *five* children had to accept a three-bedroom house—because a lieutenant with one child got the last four-bedroom house. Or we could wait a *year* to get a larger base home (it was only a seventeen-month assignment).

Stuffing five children into two bedrooms turned out not to be as challenging as bathing children in a bathtub the size of a laundry basket. The bathrooms were two feet long by two feet wide—the size of a matchbox. It was enough to drive a half-wit to caffeine-laden distractions.

One evening, Joshua and Jonathan were already bathed and dressed for bed—*two down, three to go*. The older boys were going to take their showers soon, and Bethany, also known as "Bunny," was in the tub. Bob needed some towels out of the dryer. He left Bethany unattended for a couple of minutes. She was six years old, the tub was tiny, so there was no danger of drowning. No problem, right? Wrong.

Pretty soon, we heard Bethany belt out, "MAMA, PAPA! COME HERE, QUICK!"

I ran from the kitchen and met Bob already scrambling down the hallway. We stuffed ourselves into the bathroom and saw the reason for Bunny's panic attack. Seated with her in the bathtub was seventeen-month-old Joshua—still in his pajamas.

It was one of those moments when you laugh, cry, put in your parenting resignation, or run for the camera. Bob went to get Joshua some dry clothes, while I ran for the camera. Once again, we heard our daughter: "MAMA, PAPA!"

This time, we crammed in to find Joshua, Bethany, and *Jonathan* seated in the tub—donned in his pj's. After Joshua got so much attention for his antics, three-year-old Jonathan thought he'd do the same. He wanted to be in the picture!

Daniel and Philip heard the commotion, squeezed into the tiny room, and perched on top of the toilet to watch the show. Bethany, still in her birthday suit, screamed as the older boys giggled. Seven people in a phone-booth-size space. With the boys laughing, Bunny crying, and the babies posing—I snapped pictures. Bob resigned. At least for the evening.

In order to save the most amount possible, the entire family needs to cooperate. Whether you have a family of two or ten, couponing can be a family effort. I recommend a family conference on the subject (hopefully in a space larger than that bathroom). Items on the agenda for this life-changing conference should include: team efforts, projected savings, and team goals for coupon savings.

Tips and Testimonies for Family Fun

Don't Be Brand-Specific

"Sweetheart, do you think it would be worth an extra $200 a month, or $2,400 a year, to be less brand-specific? What could our family do with that savings each year?"

This team idea is a cooperative effort encouraging everyone to do their part. Your "part" can be as simple as not complaining about certain brands. Most coupon purchases (on sale items) are brand name products. Since sales and coupon availability vary from week to week, a family cannot afford to be brand specific. In the competitive product market, most name brands are of equal quality (with few exceptions). A staunch refusal to pledge loyalty to any particular brand will save your family a lot of money.

Where Are You?

The next area, projected savings, is a topic that attracts everyone's attention. The Cost of Food at Home chart (Figure 3-A) was taken from *The Family Economics and Nutrition Review*. It provides information on the United States average per capita cost of food at home for four spending levels. To compute your family's food costs, complete the following steps:

First, add all the family's grocery receipts for the last three months. In the absence of receipts or canceled checks, estimate the expenditures. Be sure to add all those little trips to the convenience store, too.

Then divide the total by three to compute your family's monthly food costs. This figure is the average amount you spend per month on groceries.

Next, calculate your family's average spending amounts based on the criteria given on the chart. Note the use of age and gender in calculating your family's amounts. Compare your monthly spending habits with the four spending levels on the Cost of Food at Home chart.

Determine where your family falls on the chart. Are you a liberal spender? Maybe you're moderate or average in your spending habits. Or maybe you've figured a lot of this stuff out and you're already a thrifty shopper.

Cost Savings Projection

With this information, current spending levels can be compared with national averages in the four categories listed. A projected savings plan may also be computed. Using the *Shop, Save, and Share* method, your family can lower your spending level to the thrifty plan. Now that you've figured out what you can save, all you have to do is figure out what to do with that savings!

Cost of Food at Home

Figure 3-A

Cost of food at home estimated for food plans at four cost levels, March 1997, U.S. Average[1]

Sex-age group	Cost for 1 week				Cost for 1 month			
	Thrifty plan	Low-cost plan	Moderate cost plan	Liberal plan	Thrifty plan	Low-cost plan	Moderate cost plan	Liberal plan
FAMILIES								
Family of 2:[2]								
20-50 years	$56.70	$71.70	$88.30	$110.10	$245.60	$310.80	$383.10	$477.40
51 years +	53.40	69.10	86.30	102.20	231.20	299.00	369.50	442.90
Family of 4:								
Couple, 20-50 years								
and children—								
1-2 and 3-5 years	82.30	103.30	126.20	155.40	356.80	447.50	547.10	673.60
6-8 and 9-11 years	94.60	121.60	151.50	182.80	410.40	526.80	656.90	792.30
INDIVIDUALS[3]								
Child:								
1-2 years	14.80	18.20	21.30	25.80	64.10	78.80	92.20	111.90
3-5 years	16.00	19.90	24.60	29.50	69.40	86.20	106.60	127.70
6-8 years	19.70	26.40	32.90	38.30	85.50	114.40	142.50	166.00
9-11 years	23.40	30.00	38.30	44.40	101.60	129.90	166.10	192.30
Male:								
12-14 years	24.30	33.90	42.00	49.40	105.40	146.80	182.00	214.10
15-19 years	25.10	34.90	43.40	50.20	108.60	151.20	188.20	217.50
20-50 years	27.10	34.70	43.30	52.50	117.40	150.50	187.80	227.70
51 years +	24.40	33.20	40.80	49.00	105.90	143.50	176.70	212.20
Female:								
12-19 years	24.20	29.20	35.40	42.80	105.00	126.60	153.60	185.70
20-50 years	24.40	30.50	37.00	47.60	105.90	132.00	160.50	206.30
51 years +	24.10	29.60	36.70	43.90	104.30	128.20	159.20	190.40

[1]Assumes that food for all meals and snacks is purchased at the store and prepared at home. Estimates for the thrifty food plan were computed from quantities of foods published in *Family Economics Review 1984* (1). Estimates for the other plans were computed from quantities of foods published in *Family Economics Review 1983* (2). The costs of the food plans are estimated by updating prices paid by households surveyed in 1977-78 in USDA's Nationwide Food Consumption Survey. USDA updates these survey prices using information from the Bureau of Labor Statistics, CPI Detailed Report, table 4, to estimate the costs for the food plans.

[2]Ten percent added for family size adjustments. See footnote 3.

[3]The costs given are for individuals in 4-person families. For individuals in other size families, the following adjustments are suggested: 1-person–add 20 percent; 2-person–add 10 percent; 3-person–add 5 percent; 5- or-6 person –subtract 5 percent; 7- or more-person–subtract 10 percent.

It Takes So Little to Be Above Average

According to this chart, a family of seven, with children ages two to nine, spends $911.34 per month on a "moderate" or *average* spending plan (Figure 3-A). This amounts to $10,936.08 per year for *food alone!* Keep in mind the fact that these charts do not include toiletries and cleansers.

Our family of seven's monthly budget is $200. This figure *includes* toiletries, cleansers, and diapers. Since the thrifty column for our family size is $410.40 a month, you can see we spend $210.40 less *every month* than the thriftiest four-person family in the United States.

We also share the wealth with others in that $200 a month we spend. Usually, we give away nine grocery bags a month to individuals or groups. A conservative estimate of $15 a bag means we give away $135 worth of groceries each month. However, I usually spend only $5 per bag—that's why we're able to give away so much food. It's God's provision for others in need.

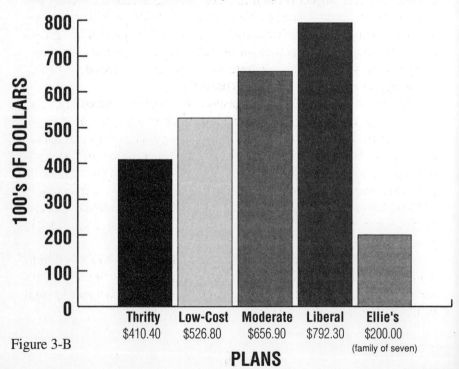

Food Costs (As Reported in *Family Economics and Nutrition Review*, March '97) Family of Four

100's OF DOLLARS

Thrifty	Low-Cost	Moderate	Liberal	Ellie's
$410.40	$526.80	$656.90	$792.30	$200.00
				(family of seven)

Figure 3-B

PLANS

Delegate, Darling!

If I'm a Coupon Queen, then I'm also a Practicality Princess. I believe teams work well together when each member contributes their own strengths. In a cooperative effort, we must be practical. A toddler may love to cut coupons—but he renders them useless in the process. Dad may be able to alphabetize coupons, but the thought of going to the grocery store terrifies him. Play to each member's strengths, and don't make fun of their weaknesses.

Determine who will cut, highlight, alphabetize, and pull expired coupons. Small children can highlight, while older children can cut and file coupons. I recommend safety scissors for small children and big children like our friend Jeff Cox, whose wife, Amy, says he regularly cuts his fingers on everything but power tools. She won't let him use scissors—so he highlights.

Savings Plan

There's an old saying in Texas, "If you aim at nothin', you'll hit it every time." This brings us to the final topic of discussion at the family conference. This subject is often the most fun—goals for the money you save. A family needs to decide how to take full advantage of their grocery savings. Each family establishes their own goals. However, it is a procedure that your family establish an overall household budget. Without a budget, your savings will evaporate into unproductive spending habits. We'll look at a workable budget in chapter 22.

The following is a list of suggestions people have shared with me. These will give you some ideas on what you can do with your savings.

Check it out, dude. Write a check directly into your savings account for the amount you've saved. For example, a typical *Shop, Save, and Share* trip to the grocery store yields a cart full of groceries. We'll assume most of the purchases were for items on sale, and the subtotal before coupons was $115—a big savings already. The coupons are presented to the checker and he deducts another $35. You could immediately write a check for $35 into your savings account.

Get out of debt. The average American family has too much consumer debt—they're slaves to their credit card masters. Many families use their savings to double up on payments. There's a tremendous amount of liberty found in being free from the bondage of debt.

Pay cash for that second car. Others save enough cash to pay for a good secondhand car. Bob and I have done that several times—just a portion of our annual savings.

What about a dream vacation? Still other families use the extra money as a vacation fund. I've heard of families who have funded trips to Hawaii, the Cayman Islands, and the Bahamas. Where does a half-wit take her family on vacation? We go camping in exotic locations such as Moundville, Alabama; Carlsbad, New Mexico; and Flintstone Village in South Dakota.

Lower your food budget inch by inch. Yet another idea is from one family I know who lowers their food budget each month as they become more proficient with the *Shop, Save and Share* plan. They've gone from spending $450 a month to $400, then down to $350, etc. They use each incremental savings to pay off credit-card debt. This family has also made a covenant that once those debts are paid, they will never become servants to consumer debt again.

Welcome home, Mom. A final example are the families who crunch the numbers and determine that Mom could quit her part-time job and stay home. To work or not to work is one of the issues for moms in our modern-day culture. I'm not going to touch that subject—it's far too complex for someone with limited gray matter. However, it's gratifying to know that *Shop, Save, and Share* has made the difference for a woman who wanted to stay home but couldn't.

He will be like a tree firmly planted by streams of water,
which yields its fruit in its season, and its leaf does not wither; and in
whatever he does, he prospers.
Psalm 1:3

CHAPTER
SIX

Never Give
a Toddler Gum and
Other Lessons

*Tips to Avoiding Coupon Disorganization
and Finding Timely Coupons*

For my birthday this past year, Bob gave me a coffee cup—to go with my chocolate. The cup had a cow on it, dressed in an apron, running after five little calves who were getting into all kinds of mischief. The caption read: *I Like Adventure, I'm a Mom*. The scene describes our lives perfectly. We live on the brink of adventure and chaos.

That coffee cup reminds me of couponing. I think we should observe certain procedures in order to avoid mass chaos. As a mama to our little herd, I've learned a few of these lessons. For example, you should never give a toddler chewing gum to stop their whining. Never allow a nine-year-old unsupervised access to the kitchen for "simple" science experiments. The last rule is the most important. Never, ever leave scissors anywhere but inside a home vault.

What's the result of ignoring these rules? Here are some scientific results:

Toddler/gum. I had to use an entire jar of peanut butter to get gum out of *all five* of my children's hair. They had to have their sandwiches with only jelly the entire next week.

Science experiments. I had permanent lime green food coloring on 75 percent of my country blue kitchen counters. There is no such thing as a simple science experiment with kids.

Unsecured scissors. I had to rush my daughter to the beauty salon. Her brothers cut off all her beautiful blond ringlets—right before we were to have a family portrait made. On this same topic, Conan cut through an electrical cord. Oh, and did I mention it was *plugged into the outlet* at the time? Plastic safety handles and his overworked guardian angel were his only salvation.

Yes, some procedures help us avoid disaster. In couponing, there are some organizational tips that help avoid mass chaos at the grocery store. These time-saving tips help us save big bucks with enough time left over to indulge in our favorite pastimes. Now, where did I put that mug?

Tips to Avoiding Coupon Disorganization

Highlight

In couponing, I've discovered a helpful procedure is to highlight the expiration dates on the coupons. This helps me avoid disaster in the grocery store. Usually these dates are located on the top of the coupon—they may already be highlighted. Sometimes, however, they are in fine print and are difficult to locate. Highlighting also saves time at the end of each month when expired coupons are removed.

Even though highlighting is considered a procedure, the *way* you do it is your own technique. Personally, I gather my three copies of each free-standing insert (FSI) and match each of the identical pages together. As you probably remember, an FSI is the coupon packet found in the Sunday paper. With these pages matched, I highlight the coupon expiration dates. I've found this saves time over cutting out coupons first, and highlighting a big pile of unruly coupons *afterward*. You will find a technique that works best for you.

After I've highlighted the matched FSI pages, I then cut the coupons. Since I matched the coupon pages, I can cut out *three* coupons by making *one* cut. I repeat this process for the rest of the FSIs, getting a three-for-one return on my time investment!

As I cut out each set of coupons, I place them on my dining room table in alphabetical piles. After all of the coupons have been cut out for the week, I gather the piles in alphabetical order. Then I am ready to file my coupons, which brings us to the next procedure.

Alphabetical Order Versus Categorical Order—Who Wins?

Your level of commitment to the *Shop, Save, and Share* system will be determined by one incredibly intense question: "Are you willing to switch from categorical to alphabetical order?" I have found that alphabetical tabs are more efficient than categorical ones. Since the categorical system is so firmly entrenched in the American way of life, I can see I may have to convince some of you.

The Proof Is in the Puddin'

Have you ever wondered what that saying means? I heard it a lot growing up. I think it means a cook can brag all they want about their special recipe—but the real proof is how the pudding tastes. Here's my proof. The most common and simple categorical systems have ten to twelve divisions. Alphabetical tabs have twenty-three divisions. The more precisely a coupon is filed, the more quickly it is found when you need it.

To show you what I mean, let's take the problem of looking for a "soap" coupon in a categorical coupon box. First, you have to find the soap section. Then you have to wade through the coupons for bar soap, liquid soap, laundry soap, and dishwashing soap before the desired *automatic* dishwasher soap coupon is located. This is a waste of time. It ain't good puddin'.

Another problem with the categorical system is the fact that it taxes your brain too much. For example, you have to remember whether you filed a milk coupon under "dairy" or "beverage." Other family members using your coupons don't know where you've filed the milk coupon either. Can you see how filing by category can be cumbersome and inefficient? Even a system with twice as many categories simply means twice as many divisions to remember. Alphabetical filing means you look at the product, see what letter it starts with, and look under that letter in your file. Simple. Give this filing system a try. You may find as you make the adjustment that you are reaping the benefits of time-saving efficiency.

While filing alphabetically is a procedure, *how* you file alphabetically is your own technique. It's a good idea for the same person who files the coupons to establish some *filing techniques*. It can be a disaster if two or three people in your family are organizing coupons with different filing systems.

The Most Prominent Name on the Coupon

I've discovered the easiest way to file coupons alphabetically is to file them by the name *most prominent on the coupon*. This name is also the most prominent on the product itself, which makes it easy to find on the grocer's shelf. For instance, *Right Guard* deodorant is filed under *R*. Also remember to file alphabetically under each letter heading. For example, in the *R* section I have the following order: Ragu, Raid, Ralston cereals, Reach toothpaste, ReaLemon juice, Red Baron pizza, etc.

By keeping them in order under each alphabetical heading, the coupon you want is very easy to locate. The exception to this rule involves big food groups.

Large Food Groups—A Master's-Level Concept

There are a few products easily located in their large food groups. For instance, Kellogg's cereal products. All Kellogg's coupons are filed in the *K* section. Since I have about two hundred Kellogg's coupons, I have them filed alphabetically within the Kellogg food group. The coupons under Kellogg's are filed alphabetically as follows: All-Bran, Apple Jacks, Bran Flakes, Corn Flakes, Corn Pops, Crispix, Cracklin' Oat Bran, etc. This allows the coupon professional easy access to desired coupons.

It may be difficult to understand large food groups until you've accumulated quite a number of coupons. Then the pattern is evident. You might want to make note of the following large food groups and file them as described above: *Betty Crocker, Duncan Hines, General Mills (cereals only), Hormel, Keebler, Kellogg's, Kraft, Oscar-Mayer, Nabisco, Pillsbury, and Louis Rich.*

You may discover other large food groups (in your region of the country) not included in this list. *Bryan* meat products are only available in certain states, and there are other regional products as well. You probably noticed General Mills *cereals* were listed as a large food group. This does not include all General Mills products, as their empire is too vast to efficiently file under one heading.

A Coupon Box Evolution Revisited

I am not a Darwinist. I don't believe in the evolution of species. However, I *do* believe in the evolution of coupon boxes. The survival of the fittest. This brings us to the next step in organizing your coupons—finding a suitable coupon box.

My first coupon box was a sweet, little three-inch tin decorated with kitty cats. It had the word "Coupons" across the top. Carrying this into the grocery store was socially acceptable. In the developmental process, the kitty-cat tin evolved into a slightly larger tin decorated with country lambs. It, too, was socially acceptable *and* politically correct.

Then the survival of the fittest took over. I forgot societal norms and took the big plunge—a shoebox-size plastic container. It served me well for about three years, until the lid fell off and my lifetime savings of coupons were blown across the parking lot in the California High Desert. I thought it was the end of life as I knew it.

Leave the Rigging to Jimmy

Soon the shoebox wasn't large enough, and it evolved into the missing link—the sweater storage box. I must admit, I have a delightful way of making things work when they usually don't. If Martha Stewart can make a sled out of weathered wood (from the old barn behind her house) and a glue gun, I could certainly fix a coupon box. I rigged the sweater box with a cardboard strip hot glued down the center. That way, coupons can be filed on either side of the strip.

My new coupon box was big. *How big?* you may ask. Well, it wouldn't fit in the child's seat of a grocery cart. *That big?* It barely fit in the trunk of my Suburban! When I proudly showed the latest box to my friend Sandy, she laughed me to scorn. I dismissed her rejection. I think she was under heavy conviction to start couponing. She took one look at the box and jeered, "That's not a *coupon* box, that's a *sweater* box."

Creatively Challenged

The next coupon box I owned reminded me of the changing seasons of life. You know, "A time to give birth, and a time to die; a time to plant, and a time to uproot what is planted; a time to make crafts, and a time to refrain from craftmaking" (Ecclesiastes 3:2, half-wit paraphrase).

This lovely coupon box was made of red-and-white striped polyester left over from kitchen curtains I made for Bob's nana. Since the sweater box was too wide, I solved the problem. The fabric box was extra long, and was surrounded by 4" flat lace. Two ribbons tied around the top of the box held it securely in place. I didn't want my (coupon) babies flying out again in the High Desert. The sides were kind of lopsided, but I patched them quite nicely. When I first reflected on this work of art, I thought it looked like a Salvation Army reject. Then I took in a tuck here and folded an edge there until I convinced myself that it looked fine.

I used that box for three years. Despite some fairly heroic rigging efforts—it fell apart. You may think I use a suitcase on wheels these days.

Actually, the coupon box I've used for the last five years is an 8" x 12" x 3" Rubbermaid box with a snap-on lid. The lid prevents spills, and the size fits easily into the child's seat of a grocery cart. That box is the last link in the evolutionary line—the survival of the fittest.

Identify Your Coupon Box

Remember to write your name on your coupon box as well as your phone number and/or address. I've talked to brokenhearted couponers who left their unmarked coupon boxes in the store—never to see them again. On the other hand, everyone I've talked to who had written their name and number on their box had it returned. Usually, if you leave your box at the store, the bag boy or checker will see it first and return it to the customer service desk. Then you'll get a phone call.

There are some fun ways to counter the monotony of clipping and organizing coupons. If the following tips are followed closely, you'll have plenty of time left over for some family fun.

Tips to Timely Coupons

Read Your Coupons Monthly

While seemingly a dreary exercise, it is absolutely crucial that you read through your box at least once a month. I read through my coupons when the children ask to watch the *Veggie Tales—Dave and the Giant Pickle* for the one hundred and fifty-sixth time. My favorite technique, however, is to put the children down for their afternoon quiet time, prepare some gourmet coffee, and eat some—you've got it—chocolate while I read through my coupons.

Sometimes, I'll take my box along when we travel an hour to see the sights of the big city of El Paso or the lovely Fort Bragg. An hour in the car, when I'm not driving, is all I need to read through all of my coupons. I look for three things when I read: expired dates, upcoming expirations, and out-of-order coupons.

Pull Expired Coupons

The first thing to look for is the expired coupon. These are easy to spot because the date has been highlighted. By removing these coupons from the box, the couponer's integrity is protected from using an expired coupon inadvertently. Send these out-of-date coupons to military friends overseas. Remember, coupons may be used up to six months past the expiration date in overseas military commissaries.

I send an average of thirty thousand coupons overseas from our current assignment to other military units. Our sister organizations in England, Germany, Italy, and Korea rejoice in the coupon care packages.

If there are no military contacts available, give the expired coupons to your small children, grandchildren, or neighborhood children. They can play grocery games with their very own coupons and learn the value of frugality at an early age.

Notice Upcoming Expirations

The second thing to look for is upcoming expirations or coupons that will expire by the end of next month. I need to stress a point here: Do not pull *every* coupon that will expire at the end of next month. On the other hand, look for coupons that will expire that you know you can use.

Watch for Frequently Purchased Items

For instance, let's say your family members are *Cheerios* fanatics. You keep them in your baby's diaper bag for a quick snack. Your toddler loves to put his fat little finger in the holes and play with them on his highchair tray. The older children make colored Cheerios necklaces for Grandma. Your slack-jawed teenager makes marshmallow treats with them. Your spouse likes them for breakfast each morning and so do your children. In our family, we go through as many as fifteen bowls of cereal each morning—or seven boxes a week.

Let's say you know you'll buy that product when you go to the store. When reading your coupons at the end of the month, you notice all of the "50¢-off" Cheerios coupons will expire at the end of the following month. The other Cheerios coupons have no expiration date, but are only 25¢ off. That's the time to pull an upcoming expiration coupon.

Put that coupon in the "Let's see" envelope (we'll define this in chapter 8). Take these coupons to the store each week of the following month—looking for the opportunity to purchase them on sale. If the coupon is used at a double-coupon store, you'll save the most money possible on those Cheerios.

Also Watch for High-Value Coupons

Another upcoming expiration coupon to look for is the high-value coupon. These could have a great return on your time investment. For example, Pritikin came out with a healthy soup a few years ago. They ran a "50¢-off" coupon to advertise their new product. I clipped the coupon, added it to my grocery list, and went to a double-coupon store to check the price on the soup. After all, $1.00 off a can of soup could be a very good bargain.

The Pritikin product was not yet in the stores, so I put the coupon back into my "Let's see" envelope and repeated the process the next week. This pattern continued for several weeks. Still I asked, "Where's the soup?" I was frustrated when I saw pictures of the soup advertised on the grocery cart—but no soup in the store!

Finally I took the coupon out of my "Let's see" envelope and refiled it in my main alphabetical file. The month before the coupon expired, while sipping coffee and looking for *upcoming expirations*, I noticed the Pritikin coupon. Since it would expire the next month, I put it back into my "Let's see" envelope. That week, I saw Pritikin soup on the shelf at a regular price of $1.89 per can. Now it was on sale for $1.19 a can. The 50¢-off coupon I had was doubled.

Here's how it looked:

$1.89	regular price (never pay this price)
- .70	sale savings (buying on sale saved 35%)
$1.19	
- .50	coupon savings (saves an additional 25%)
- .50	double coupon store (saves another 25%)
$0.19	total price paid (a savings of 85%)

I had six coupons, so I purchased six cans of soup at nineteen cents per can. This may sound like an exceptional buy, but with the *Shop, Save, and Share* system, it's the norm. People who regularly follow this method routinely enjoy this kind of savings.

Quantity Purchases—for Master's Program Students Only

A note about quantity purchases. Some states allow a quantity limit on the number of items a customer may purchase on sale and/or with a coupon. These quantity limitations vary from store to store. It's wise to check with the store manager to clarify their policies before you shop.

For example, some stores only allow three coupons to be doubled on three *like items*. In this case, I could only buy three cans of soup, using three coupons. I could not get the double coupon benefit on cans four, five, and six. Another option with these limitations is to buy three cans now and three cans on another shopping trip.

Sometimes stores only allow a specific quantity on sale items, with additional purchases at the regular price. Pay attention to these quantity limitations and buy accordingly for maximum savings. One final quantity limitation is sometimes listed on a store coupon. It may read: "25¢ off Campbell's soup with coupon. Limit four."

This means the store will take 25¢ off four cans of soup when you present the coupon. However, remember that coupons read as a legal agreement. In this case, you *could* use two of those store coupons and get 25¢ off eight cans of soup because the coupon did not specifically stipulate, "Limit four cans per coupon and limit one coupon per customer."

Remember that combining the above mentioned store coupons with manufacturer's coupons saves even more. You could use one store coupon off each of four cans of soup in conjunction with four manufacturer's coupons to multiply the savings—if your store allows the combination. At any rate, pay special attention to quantity limitations.

Summary of Upcoming Expirations

In summarizing the section on reading upcoming expirations, remember a couple of points. You do not pull every coupon set to expire at the end of next month. However, high-value coupons (such as the Pritikin soup example) and coupons on frequently purchased products (such as the Cheerios example) should be pulled. It is very frustrating to fail to take advantage of a good coupon before its expiration date.

Order, Please!

The final area to check when reading coupons at the end of the month is for coupon order. Sometimes coupons get stuck together in the original filing process, and these misplaced coupons turn up at this time.

BEWARE—
The Grocery Nomad

Tips to an Organized List

Have you ever felt that you *should* do something, but you just didn't want to do it? There are times I feel I should give up chocolate. Then I rationalize, *I could give up chocolate, but I'm no quitter!* I had a friend who felt she should use coupons but just didn't want to do it—she thought it would be a hassle. The more she ignored the feeling deep down that she should get control of this area, the more guilty she felt. It was a terrible place to be— caught in the middle of a choice and a conviction.

One day the conviction got the better of her—she decided to do something about it. Had she ever been to a coupon seminar? No. Did she ask me for some organizational tips and ideas? No. Did she at least make a list? Once again— NO. These were her first mistakes.

She dropped her two girls off at our house to be baby-sat while she went to the store. It was then that I noticed her second mistake—she had her husband with her.

Now, before the National Center for Fathering accuses me of gender bashing, let me clarify something. I am not saying that taking a well-informed, supportive male to the store is a bad idea. Taking your average "I don't understand why you can't do better at the grocery store," or "Just go to the store and buy it" type of male can be a disaster.

Tim and Sandy left their children at our house at 7:00 P.M. They said they'd be back in an hour. They only had a few things to buy. At 11:00 P.M. their girls were asleep on our couches. Bob and I were worried.

Bob was about to go look for them when we heard an agitated knock. We opened the door to a woman emotionally on the edge and her singularly unimpressed husband.

"Are you guys all right?" Bob asked, "Did you have an accident or something?"

Tim rolled his eyes, "We had an accident all right. It began when Sandy decided she was taking her basket of coupons to the store—to try and save us some money."

I was confused. "But, Sandy, you don't use coupons, remember? You've never even been to a seminar. You *make fun* of my coupon box. Did you say a *basket* of coupons?"

The story slowly unfolded. She had two hundred coupons piled in a basket. They were not in alphabetical order. They weren't even in categorical order. The worst thing was, she had no list.

When they went to the store and saw a tag for something on sale, they sorted through all of the coupons before they went on to the next item on sale. Most of the time they could not find a coupon for the product. It took them three hours to buy $15.00 dollars worth of groceries and save $2 in coupons.

They were so flustered by the time they reached the check-out that Sandy was near the breaking point. You've heard of "the straw that broke the camel's back"? Well, an unsuspecting checker dropped that straw.

The California girl rang up the groceries and began processing the few coupons. She held out a coupon. "Like, duh, this is a *Kellogg's* Raisin Bran coupon. Hello? We *totally* cannot use it. Because, like, you got *Post* Raisin Bran." That was the straw.

Grabbing two handfuls of her own hair, Sandy gritted her teeth and tried to talk, "Did you say *Post* Raisin Bran?" Her eyes were wild with despair.

The girl knew that some people were really, like, uh, weird about their coupons. But this was, like, *too* much.

The moral of this story is threefold: (1) If you are not prepared to use coupons at the store, then DON'T USE THEM. Don't feel guilty; leave them at home with complete freedom. (2) If your spouse knows more about biking than couponing, LEAVE HIM AT HOME.

The third moral to this story is best illustrated by a major credit card motto. (3) When it comes to your list—DON'T LEAVE HOME WITHOUT

IT! Preparations for big savings continue as we learn to get the all-important list ready.

Tips to an Organized List

The Hope Diamond

Every week, in every big-city and most small-town newspapers, a marvelous find is discovered. What is this treasure? Why, it's the weekly sale circular, of course. This is a vital element in shopping preparedness. Call the local newspaper and ask them what day the grocery stores advertise their sales—then buy that day's paper. It's usually on Tuesday or Wednesday. The Sunday paper is purchased for the coupons. The midweek paper is purchased for the sale ads, although it sometimes runs some paper coupons as a bonus.

I'm Singin' in the Rain

When shopping, remember to take the sale circular to the store in order to guarantee sale prices and secure rain checks. Rain checks are issued by the grocery store when they are out of the advertised sale item. Some stores refer to them as "call-back slips" or "price guarantees." Basically, this slip of paper allows the purchase of an out-of-stock sale item at the sale price when it is eventually restocked.

Most rain checks are good for thirty days after the date of issue. Others are only good for two weeks. Be sure to use them before they expire. Also check the expiration date on coupons that will be used with the rain check, so you can take full advantage of the advertised sale and of the coupon savings.

Some stores go one step further—they guarantee their sales. If they are out of the product and you secure a rain check, the next time you're in the store you get the first sale item free and the rest at the sale price. Those are the times I find myself hoping they're out of the sale item.

Where in the World Are We?

While at the customer service desk, pick up an aisle order chart. They are also known as store directories or guides to the layout of the store. If your store does not carry these guides, suggest they develop one as a customer service aid. In the competitive grocery market industry, most managers are open to helpful ideas.

If nothing is available, then write down the aisle numbers and product headings the next time you're in the store. These product headings, or signs, are usually found hanging directly over the aisle. They display the aisle number and list the products found in that aisle. For example:

AISLE 1
FLOUR, SUGAR, BAKING NEEDS,
COFFEE, TEA, SPICES, OIL

This may take a little time on your initial trip to the store, but your time investment will have a great return. This little gem will save you lots of frustration in the future.

Saving on a Rare Commodity—TIME

A sale circular and an aisle order chart help you prepare your list at home and save TIME. Couponing is not our life. We have a wonderful life we want to enjoy. We have a life that consists of red snow cone juice on gray carpets. Children who ask the mailman, "If you walk so much with the mail, then why is your stomach hanging over your belt like that?" And a husband who doesn't even know what a measuring spoon is, much less where to find it.

Preparing at home saves time in and out of the grocery store so we can enjoy life.

Make Your List According to Aisle Order

The next step must be followed carefully. Make a pot of decaffeinated hazelnut coffee. Cut one chocolate cherry brownie. Then sit at the kitchen table with your coupon box, a pen, a calculator, the sale circular, and the aisle order chart. Finally, write the week's grocery list according to aisle order. A list is a procedure; *how* you make a list is up to your personal technique. Coffee and brownies are a procedure. The flavor of the coffee is your own technique. A good place to start is with the sales.

A Mind Is a Terrible Thing to Waste—Use a Calculator

While sipping your coffee and nibbling on a brownie, you look at the first page of this week's sale circular. Yoplait yogurt is advertised at 3/$1.00 You find your coupon for "50¢ off five," which will be doubled. My quick mind (i.e., a calculator) figures five yogurts will cost $1.66 minus the coupon savings of $1.00. Each individual yogurt will cost 66¢ divided by five, for a total of 13¢ each.

That's a good buy. Write it on your list in aisle order and pull all other

Yoplait coupons from your coupon box. This method in making a list keeps you organized and saves time in the store. The more coupons we gather at home before shopping, the less time we spend in the store. The less time we spend in the store, the more money we save.

Look for Bonus Sizes

Moving to page two of the sale circular, you notice a 16 oz. bottle of Alberto VO5 shampoo advertised for 89¢. Recently, they've had specially marked bottles of VO5—"20 oz. for the price of 16 oz." This shampoo also comes in a baby shampoo variety. You find a 35¢-off coupon that will be doubled. So you can get a 20 oz. bottle of baby shampoo for 19¢. I could donate some of those to a local orphanage.

Sold. Write the product and sale price in aisle order on your grocery list, pull the manufacturer's coupon, and write down the quantity you'll buy. The quantity is determined by how many coupons you have and the store's quantity limits.

You should routinely look for larger bonus sizes of products on the shelf. They are usually located beside the regular-size item, but you'll get more for your money. By the way, you can't get rain checks on bonus-size items—so buy them while they're available.

Sometimes an item on sale and with a coupon will cost more than I am willing to pay, so I don't buy it. Each purchase is evaluated and each price assessed on an individual basis. This process is repeated with everything in the sale circular.

Master's Technique—The Limited List

In place of a full grocery list, I use a limited list instead. This is a time-saving technique I developed years ago, and it still works. I don't write every item on my grocery list. Instead, I use my coupons as reminders. I still write the sale items and prices on a list, but I do not write the items for which I have a coupon. I place the product coupon in the proper place in the coupon envelope (see next chapter). The coupon's presence reminds me I need to purchase that item.

This saves time over writing every item I need on an extensive list. I only write items on my grocery list for which I do not have a coupon. The coupons, arranged in aisle order in the coupon envelope, are taken to the store, along with the coupon box for the big shop.

Ask and Ye Shall Receive

Occasionally, there are a few items not found on an aisle order chart. When in doubt, ask a stocker, checker, or store manager where the item is located. If it is a frequently purchased item, note it on your aisle order chart. If they are out of the item on the shelf and it's on sale, there are oftentimes special displays of these sale items at the front of the store or on an endcap. Endcaps are located at the end of the aisles. I usually ask the store personnel to take me to the display or show me the item on the shelf. This also saves time and endless wandering. There's an additional advantage to a well-prepared list—you'll avoid becoming a grocery nomad.

The Grocery Nomad

Webster's dictionary defines a nomad as "one of a people that has no fixed location but roams from place to place. An individual who wanders aimlessly." Did you know there's also a grocery nomad?

We've all seen members of this tribe of people in the grocery store. The first thing you notice about a nomad is that their cart is usually full. Second, you'll see a vacant, puzzled look on their face. You may hear guttural muttering, "Oh no! I forgot...to get...peanut butter. Now, where is the...OOOGA-OOOGA...peanut butter?"

In the early stages of nomadic wandering, people of this tribe are harmless. When they enter stage two, however, you need to use extreme caution. It's safest to look straight into the eyes of a nomad to determine their threat level. These barbarians are chock-full of potential danger. When you see their eyes light up—BEWARE! They have just hit the realization stage.

They may release an uncivilized war cry when realization hits them. Their piercing screams can be heard throughout the store. "PEA-NUT. BUT-TER. PEANUT BUTTER! AISLE 17."

In the final stages of nomadic wanderings, grocery nomads have been clocked at 25 mph. They will push a full cart of groceries, wielding it as a weapon, running into and over unwary shoppers. Their main goal is to bag their kill (the peanut butter) and get to the check-out before they waste any more time in the store. They don't care about the cost. They're frustrated. They just want their freedom—at any price.

Don't let this happen to you. Write your list in aisle order and you will not be vulnerable to this barbaric behavior. After all, it's not just an illness—it's a way of life.

A Bad-Hair Day and Other Offenses

Tips to an Organized Coupon Envelope

I've lived and shopped all over the United States—I may come shopping in your town one day. Imagine what it's like to see me in action at the check-out. What if you got in my line?

After my groceries have been scanned and the checker is beginning to deduct coupons, it appears—to the average shopper—that I'm almost finished. You see, when I'm on a "regular" shop (and not a "short" shop) it usually takes a good checker twenty minutes to deduct my coupons. It's worth the wait. A technique I regularly follow, as should you, is to warn people in line behind me.

One time I went to the grocery store and got in the line of my favorite checker—Heather. The last few products were on the grocery belt when an older woman with eight items walked up behind me. As I would soon discover, this lady had an attitude.

Courtesy demanded that I warn her. "Excuse me, ma'am. I have a lot of coupons. You would probably get checked out faster if you went to the express line."

Still holding her vegetables above the grocery belt, the woman stared at me in disbelief. I didn't understand her annoyed facial expression. *I haven't been in this town long, but don't they talk to folks in line in this state? I was polite, wasn't I?*

Whatever the case, I was sure of one thing—I had offended her.

She snapped, "I use coupons, too." As if to make her point, she adjusted the net on her gray hair bun with a firm shake, and waved a Geritol coupon under my nose.

With angry determination, she continued placing her produce on the belt.

I smiled my sweetest little-girl smile. Maybe she'd like me better if she thought of me as a granddaughter. "I'm sure you do, but I *really* use coupons. It's going to take the checker a long time to deduct all of them." I held up my coupon envelope to show her.

It didn't work. I was totally unprepared for her emotional response. She gave me a ferocious glare, shaking her zucchini at me like a samurai warrior, and said coldly through clenched teeth, "I told you. I USE COUPONS, TOO!"

Well, she needn't be quite so direct—I got the point. I wondered if it was against the law to wield a zucchini as a deadly weapon? I decided to leave her alone to enjoy her bad-hair day in solitude.

As Heather scanned my last few items, the older woman *seethed* at the "audacity of young people these days." She arranged and rearranged her produce and vitamins on the conveyor belt.

Heather had not heard the verbal assault at the other end of her line. "Ellie, can I have your coupons now?"

I walked around the corner to Heather and handed her the contents of my coupon envelope. The woman with an attitude looked somewhat *surprised* at the pile of coupons.

Heather looked down at the big pile and whispered confidentially to the lady, "Ellie really does use coupons! We call her the Coupon Queen!" She began ringing in one coupon after another—and another—and another—and another.

The lady's face showed *frustration*; she hadn't realized I had *so many* coupons. Then *confusion* set in. Should she pick up her veggies and change lanes? Or should she stay where she was? *Resolution* settled into her thin features as she seemed to reason, *I'll just stay put. How much longer can it be?*

Another five minutes, and *wonder* crept into her face. She couldn't stand it. She broke the silence, "Have I seen you on *Oprah*?"

She straightened her hair. "Are you one of those people who buys all kinds of groceries for next to nothing?" She was openly *curious* now.

After Heather finished, Mrs. Hairbun asked, "Well, how much did she save anyway?"

The checker proudly announced, "The bill was around $150 and she paid $50, so she saved over $100."

She looked me in the face and stared in *awe.*

As I turned to leave, she put a staying hand on my arm, "You're *right,* girl. YOU USE COUPONS!"

One last emotion flickered in her eyes. I think it was *humility.*

Tips to an Organized Coupon Envelope

Coupon Envelope

In getting your list ready, the *coupon envelope* plays an essential role in organization and in saving time. A letter-size, plain envelope makes the best coupon envelope. You should use different envelopes for each store you visit, and you may want to write the name of the grocery store on the outside of it. (I reuse mine over and over.) The envelope contains your shopping list, the store and manufacturer's coupons you selected when you made your list (see below and chapter 7), and the "Let's see" coupons (defined earlier and below).

I keep the coupon envelope in my coupon box for easy access. As I make a list according to sale items, I pull the appropriate coupon and place it in aisle order in the coupon envelope. If the coupons are in aisle order inside the envelope, it's easier to use them properly in the store. For example, when I get to my favorite store, the first aisle I see contains canned vegetables. Since Del Monte has tomatoes on sale at 2/$1.00, the *50¢-off four* coupons are the first coupons in my envelope. The Bush's baked beans coupons are next in the envelope, and so on.

"Let's See" Coupons

All store coupons, manufacturer's coupons, and "Let's see" coupons intended for your shopping trip should be included in the coupon envelope. "Let's see" coupons are those coupons meeting one of two criteria. (1) They have a high value when doubled. (2) They are coupons for needed items; you're taking them to the store to "see" whether they are a good bargain or not.

High-Value Coupons

"Let's see" coupons that have a high value when doubled may allow you to get an item for pennies or even for free. For example, when cutting the Sunday FSI coupons, I saw Franco-American's coupon for 50¢

off a new product: *Superiore Pasta*. When doubled, this coupon is $1.00 off one can of pasta.

I included this coupon as a "Let's see" coupon, filed in aisle order in the coupon envelope. In the store, my goal was to price this product—to see if the price was right. Its regular price was $1.29, which made it 29¢. Ordinarily, I'd wait until it went on sale for 99¢, and get it free.

But we were going camping this weekend. Pasta meals make great lunches for the kids. We have meaningful family bonding time on these trips, while experiencing the great outdoors with five clones of Calvin and Hobbes. Because I sometimes live dangerously, I bought them at FULL PRICE! Even the Coupon Queen makes an occasional exception.

Needed-Item Coupons

The "Let's see" category also includes coupons for needed items. When you prepare a list, there will inevitably be items that are not advertised in the sale circular. Let's say, in theory, I might have a need for laundry soap—since I do fourteen loads of laundry each week. We'll also say there's no soap advertised this week in the sale circular. I have no idea which brand is the best bargain. So I'll pull coupons for all the laundry soap brands I can think of—Wisk, Tide, Surf, Ajax, Gain, All, Purex, and Cheer. I file these coupons in aisle order in the coupon envelope. I make sure to select the highest coupon value (when doubled) as well as the ones with the nearest expiration date.

When I go to the laundry soap section in the grocery store, I'll pull out all the soap coupons and determine which box is the best value. This week, a large box of Surf, regularly $9.99, has an unadvertised sale of $6.99. I have a 75¢-off-one coupon, which will be doubled. I'll pay $5.49 for the box of Surf, the best buy, per ounce, in the store. Oh goody, now I get to go home and do laundry—be still, my heart.

Buy One/Get One Free—The Master's Course

The above Surf example was not a theoretical story—it really happened. Furthermore, when I went to the store that week, they had a 48-hour special. The $6.99 soap was now "BUY ONE, GET ONE FREE."

This made the soap $3.50 per box. There are two ways a store's cash register computer scans the *buy one/get one free* items. (1) It marks each item half price—$3.49 for the first box and $3.50 for the second box. (2) It scans the first item at full price ($6.99), and the second free ($.00).

In the first example, when each item is half price, I can buy three, instead of four, and still get the half price benefit. Better than that, when an item is scanned at half price, I can use a coupon for *each item* purchased, even though one of the items is supposed to be free. In this case, I used a 75¢ coupon (doubled) on a box of soap marked $3.50 and paid $2.00 per box.

In the second example, the register scans the first box of soap at full price ($6.99) and scans the second at $.00. In this case, I can only use a coupon for the first item. So, I'd pay $6.99 less a seventy-five cent (doubled) coupon for a total of $5.49 for two boxes, or $2.75 per box. As you can see, the first example allows me the better bargain at $2.00 per box.

Ask the store manager how his registers scan the buy one, get one free items. Their policy can make the difference in where you shop and how you shop. I've seen it both ways in the same town. Incidentally, when I got the $2.00 per box bargain, the store had a limit of "two offers per customer." So I was only able to get four mega-size boxes—they lasted me two months.

After I purchased the Surf soap, I took the other "Let's see" coupons (for the brands I didn't use) and put them in the back of the coupon box. These coupons and others that I don't use will be refiled alphabetically at a later time. This keeps coupons out of the coupon envelope that you did not use—it keeps you honest and it keeps you organized.

Arrange Coupon Envelope in Aisle Order

As I mentioned, to stay organized and save time in the store, you need to arrange your coupon envelope in aisle order. Begin with the coupons for items in aisle one, and so on. For example, let's say the first item I see on aisle one is CornNuts. They were regularly $1.49 and are on sale for 99¢. A coupon worth 40¢ off will be doubled for a total of 80¢ off. This makes the price of CornNuts only 19¢. I have four coupons, so I buy four canisters.

I move the CornNuts coupons from the front of the coupon envelope to the back, and those items are placed in the cart. The coupon envelope is arranged in aisle order so time isn't wasted looking for these coupons. The same process is followed for the next coupon in the envelope, and so on until I finish the big shop.

When I get to the last aisle in the store, the CornNuts coupons will, once again, be at the front of the envelope. This indicates three things. (1) All my grocery items have been located and are in the cart. (2) Every coupon in the coupon envelope matches up with a product in the basket.

(3) I'm ready to give the contents of the coupon envelope to the checker.

If I am using the limited-list technique, I'll have all the coupons needed in the coupon envelope. If the limited-list technique is still unclear, don't worry. Just remember, it's a master's-level tip. Use what you can and reread this section later.

Check Off Found Items/Mark Free Items

This is going to sound so simple. Maybe it's because I'm a half-wit, but it took me a couple of years to figure out this tip. A couple of years' worth of work deserves at least a paragraph in this chapter.

When using a list, whether a regular list or a limited list, be sure to mark off items that have been placed in the grocery cart. Just place a mark through the item on your list so you know you've got it. It's surprising how much time you can save by marking items off a list.

If items are not marked off the list, then you must search the entire list each time you look at it to see where you are on your list! You have to find which product in the shopping trip comes next. For instance, the shopper looks at the list and thinks, *I got lettuce, tomatoes, bananas; I need grapes.* After the best grapes are placed in the basket, the entire process must be repeated. "I got lettuce, tomatoes, bananas, grapes; I need *carrots.*"

Life is too short to waste time going over a list like this. Use a pen, use a pencil, use a crayon, use a lipstick tube, whatever—but *mark the items off.*

Keep that pen to mark another item in the store—free items. Sometimes a coupon will state: "Free Trial Size of New Listerine Toothpaste." The tube of toothpaste is 69¢. There is usually a place on the coupon to write in the price. It is indicated as "Write the price here."

Another free-item coupon may read: "Buy One Glad Sandwich Bags/Get One Snack Bags Free." After you buy the sandwich bags, you'll need to write the price of the snack bags in the space provided. Most checkers and managers appreciate the prices written on the coupon. This saves the checker the time it takes to look over an *entire* receipt to locate the price of *one* item. It also saves you time in the grocery store.

Coupons on Buy One/Get One Free—A Master's Concept

If you have a "buy one/get one free" *manufacturer's* coupon, in most cases, a manufacturer's coupon *cannot* be used on the qualifying item. In the Glad bag example, the fine print in the coupon stated, "Limit one coupon per purchase. No other manufacturer's coupon may be used in conjunction with this coupon." I could not use a coupon on the sandwich bags when I was using a coupon to get the snack bags free.

On the other hand, remember that two *different* kinds of coupons may *usually* be used on the same item with the limitations previously expressed in chapter 4. For example, when a store coupon offers a free item, the store coupon can be used in conjunction with a manufacturer's coupon. If the Glad bag "buy one/get one free" was a store coupon, I could use a manufacturer's coupon on the qualifying purchase—the sandwich bags. The snack bags would still be free as part of the store coupon.

Here's another illustration. Last week I went to the grocery store and had a *manufacturer's* coupon that read: "Buy One Certs/Get One Free." My coffee-and-chocolate breath can use some help now and then, so I bought two rolls of Certs and used only one coupon. I couldn't use my *manufacturer's* "25¢-off" coupon on the first roll of Certs I bought.

That same shopping trip, I had a *store coupon* that read, "$1 off bread when you buy three Campbell's soups." The soup was on sale 3/$1, and I had a *manufacturer's* coupon for "25¢ off three." The store offered double coupons, so I bought three cans of soup for 50¢ and got a 79¢ loaf of bread free.

Coupon Envelope Order

I give my coupon envelope to the checker either before or after the groceries have been scanned, depending upon the store policy and the checker. I have it organized for their convenience. First in the coupon envelope are the store coupons. They are usually rung in under a special key and filed separately.

The second group of coupons in the coupon envelope is the free-item coupons with the prices indicated. There are usually only a few of each of these first two categories of coupons. The final group of coupons in the envelope is the regular manufacturer's coupons. This last section is usually still in aisle order.

This is the extent to which the coupon envelope needs to be organized. Some people have tried to separate all the 50¢ and 25¢ manufacturer's coupons. This takes a lot of *your* time and saves the checker *no* time. She still has to scan or enter the required key for these coupons individually. It wastes time to organize the envelope any further.

Mega Adventures Unlimited, Inc.

Tips to Simple and Profitable Refunding

A few years ago we headed out to Carlsbad Caverns for more vacation fun. I was amazed after the first couple of days. I thought, *I just can't believe it! Nothing happened this weekend. Jonathan didn't take off a full diaper and decorate the hotel room. Bethany didn't color the hotel walls with her markers. Philip didn't even ask the waitress rude questions about her orange hair.*

Of course, that type of fortune is bound to change. At the caverns we chose to take the four-mile walking tour amid the glorious underground beauty. About twenty feet into the tour, Jonathan and Joshua decided they had walked enough, so Bob and I each carried a baby for the next three and nine-tenths miles. A mile into the trip, Joshua loaded his diaper, so we stopped in the *King's Palace* room and changed him by a stalagmite. One and one-half miles into the trip, Jonathan did the same. This time, it was so bad he trashed out his clothes *and Bob's*—since he was the lucky one carrying him. So we stopped in the *Queen's Chamber* and changed him near a stalactite.

Two miles into the trip, Daniel announced he had to go, too.

We had a problem. A BIG problem. We were exactly halfway into a circular tour—the only rest rooms were two miles ahead or two miles back.

Daniel started to dance. "I really got to go, Mom!"

"Daniel, I know you're uncomfortable, but the nearest bathrooms are two miles away."

"You're going to have to hold it," Bob announced when Daniel whined again.

As we continued, Daniel started to turn blue and jump around. We were near the Bottomless Pit and I was concerned for his safety.

It was not like we were in the woods and he could head off behind a bush.

All of a sudden, a light bulb went off in my head. *The diaper bag, of course!*

Making sure traffic was blocked on the path in both directions, I put a diaper down on the floor of the caverns next to a stalactite column. Daniel took aim and cleared his vision. We put the wet diaper into the trash can.

My son's life was saved, he didn't fall into the Bottomless Pit, and our family adventure continued with Daniel enjoying the beauty and fascination of the caverns. *Life is so good.*

Your life may not be a perpetual adventure; you may live the average life I only dream about. On the other hand, you may have the blood of a fighter pilot, sky diver, or spelunker running through your veins. Whatever the current level of excitement in your life—I'm about to provide the opportunity for more.

When done correctly and well, refunding can provide the icing on your savings cake. Now, *that's* a great adventure!

Tips to Simple and Profitable Refunding

The Adventure Continues

The adventure in savings does not end with savings *inside* the grocery store. The adventure continues with savings *outside* the grocery store. The *Shop, Save, and Share* system stands alone and does not require refunding in order to be effective. However, a greater savings is realized if you can organize refunds. Defined, refunds are simply offers from the manufacturer for money back, coupons for free items, or gifts and other products. The conditions and limitations of the refund agreement must be met—to the letter.

Not All Refunds Are Created Equal

Not all refunds are good bargains. You must consider your time investment, postage, and stationery as well. Unlike coupons, you won't clip and save *every* refund. Some refunds are for 50¢ cash back or even 75¢ cash back. My *technique* is—I don't bother with these. By the time I consider my time investment, the 32¢ stamp, and the envelope—I'm in the red! I usually require the refunds to be at least $1.00.

Some of the items you can receive through manufacturers are good bargains. I've received a disposable camera for $1.50 postage and handling and that's cheaper than I can buy the film. Look very closely at the handling fees you have to pay for these gift items. Carefully consider each offer to determine if the price is right.

POP

Refunders speak their own language—just like fighter pilots and two-year-olds. Refunds usually require some proof of purchase, or a POP. Read the terms of the refund offer carefully to determine the required POP. Oftentimes, it is the UPC bar code on the product, but not always. I've seen POPs as anything from a foil seal on a bottle of oil to a plastic rip band on a can of juice.

It's important to determine these POPs ahead of time, so you don't throw away a major part of your qualifier. Which brings me to another refunder's term.

Qualifiers

All refunds have certain qualifiers, or terms of the agreement. A qualifier is the item required by the manufacturer to get the refund. The most common qualifiers are a receipt and a UPC (as the POP). Sometimes they can be as simple as a form on the product—with no receipt or additional POP required. Other times they are very involved, requiring three or four different items to complete the qualifier for the refund.

The extent of the qualifier will also be a determining factor for the refunds in which you choose to participate. A qualifier is something you should carefully consider—is it worth your time?

File Alphabetically

Just as in couponing, refunding is best organized alphabetically in a medium-sized box. You'll need to review your refunds once a month to make sure they don't expire before you can take advantage of them. I also file my POPs alphabetically in an envelope, paper clipped to the refund offer. That way, they're organized in one central location.

I've printed a refund checklist (Figure 4) for you to copy and keep in the front of your refund box. This list shows the date you mailed the rebate, the amount of the rebate (or gift item), the address of the manufacturer, and the date you received your refund in the mail. There is an example on the first line to give you the general idea. This is an excellent tracking mechanism to determine the value of your refunding efforts. You'll see a pattern develop and determine which rebates work best for your family.

"Read" Your Refunds

As with your coupons, at the end of each month you'll need to "read" through your refunds. You'll pull out the upcoming expirations, fulfill any completed contracts and mail them, and remove the expired offers.

Expiration Dates

Almost all refunds have an expiration date. You should highlight these dates for ease of organization at the end of the month. Most refunds are contracted to firms that process the refunds for the manufacturer. Oftentimes they'll have a special post office box for a particular offer. After the expiration date on the refund, these boxes close and your refund request will be returned unopened. Occasionally, this will not be the case. At any rate, pay attention to the expiration dates and don't waste your time or postage on an expired offer.

General Examples

Last year there was a refund offer: "Three Free Boxes of General Mills Cereals with 7 POPs." Since I only paid around 75¢ a box for most of these cereals, I had all of the qualifiers and there were no receipts required—this offer was definitely worth my time! I got $12 worth of cereal coupons for free boxes.

On the other hand, there was a cereal company that offered a watch for $14.99 plus 2 UPC codes. I will not pay that much for a watch.

REFUND CHECKLIST

MANUFACTURER'S NAME	ADDRESS	VALUE	DATE MAILED	TIME SPECIFIED	DATE RECEIVED
SAMPLE: Kool-Aid	P.O. Box 5507 Maple Plain, MN 55593	Free Mini Basketball	2/9	6-8 weeks	4/3

Figure 4

Waiting on Your Refund

Many of the refund agreement slips will indicate the amount of time you can expect to wait for your refund. Make a note on your checklist, so you'll know when to start looking for your check or product. Allow six to eight weeks in most cases.

Have a Plan

As we've discussed earlier, it's best to have a family plan for these refund perks. You may want to deposit each of the refund checks in a special savings account. I order some of the better value products as gifts for the children's birthdays and stocking stuffers for Christmas. It's a great way to relieve some of the stress of holiday buying.

You may want to turn over the cash refunding to an older child. Let them gather the qualifiers, mail the refund in, and collect the check. It is a wonderful way of teaching them the value of a dollar. One last idea: you may want to deposit your checks in a vacation account. You could have a wonderful family adventure while visiting some place like, uh—Carlsbad Caverns? Just skip the Cokes and you'll be fine.

Save

I began planning this section to be a reference guide to saving on everything from clothing and credit cards to entertainment and energy. But you know what they say about "best laid plans." My writing agenda was just interrupted by a national emergency. To give you the feel for the crisis as it unfolded, I'll reprint a portion of the emergency email I sent to friends and family.

January 8, 1998

Hi friends,

Ironically, the kids and I were watching The Man From Snowy River *and* Return From Snowy River *just before all our power went out from an ice storm. Let me explain what I mean when I say ice storm, because I've never seen anything like it. The ice adheres to everything outside and just keeps getting thicker. By the time the storm was over, a willow branch looked like a two by four. The knobs on the snowblower, normally the size of a Ping-Pong ball, are now the size of large grapefruit.*

We can't believe the damage. The experts project the area will be completely out of power anywhere from five days to four weeks. They've declared the situation a state *disaster—I've declared it a homebound bummer. Still, there is much to be thankful for at the Kay Relief Station. Other people have phone lines down, but ours is fine—for now. I'm writing on the battery power of my computer so I don't know how long this email will be. If I stop midsentence—don't worry, I'm not dead. But my battery is. Everything has literally ground to a frozen halt—overnight.*

On the other hand, we can count our blessings. We still have butane gas on the stove top and in the oven. While others have no water, we do—so we make lots of General Foods coffee to celebrate the moments of our lives. I still have a good store of chocolate from Germany that my friend Elke sent. (Thank the Lord for staples!) We have plenty of sweaters, wool socks, and blankets. With my commitment to Shop, Save, and Share, *we have enough food to last a year; Bob is here and not deployed to Bosnia—and we have candles. Our freezer is packed tight enough to keep food-stuffs frozen for a few days. After that, all we have to do is put the frozen food in the backyard—it'll keep. Of course, it may also look like giant ice balls.*

I thought I listened when God said, "Slow down." Perhaps I didn't realize just how s-l-o-w He wanted me to go.

Love from the literal frozen north,
Ellie

As you can imagine, this ice storm gives me much to think about as I write this book. I'm so glad I have enough food saved to feed our family—and others as well. This was to be one of the main points of this book, anyway, as you've probably already fig-ured out—when you save money, you're also in a position to help others. Not to mention having emergency rations always on hand.

Oops—the battery is running low. The drama of the Ice (Coupon) Queen will have to be continued.

A Penny Saved Is a Dollar Earned

Tips on the Benefits of Saving Pennies and Saving on Housing

January 9, 1998

Dear friends,
    We'd like to continue the daily saga of Kay Family Living. When last heard from, our heroes were in the midst of the worst ice storm in forty years in the North Country. Today, at 3:00 A.M., we find the Kay family delirious with joy—they have electricity again. Since the Kays are diligent people (and somewhat compulsive), they're washing ten loads of laundry, baking four loaves of bread, and doing two loads of dishes. The reason they are awake and on active duty at such an awful hour? The power came on at midnight and will probably fail again with tonight's predicted storm. They are making hay while the sun (or in this case, light bulbs) shines.
    The President of the United States has declared the North Country a National Disaster Area. Colonel Kay is working from dusk till dawn, setting up temporary shelters and rendering assistance to his people and their families. Ellie Kay has taken on the incredible challenge of keeping five children away from ten candles. The mathematical rendering? A fifty-to-one chance a child will burn his or her finger at any given moment.
    Can this situation get any worse? Can our family in crisis cope with the difficulties of falling trees, no power, no mail or phone, a

friend's fragrant dog, and children with cabin fever?

As Mama sits down to read Jonathan (aka Sweetpea) a story, he begins scratching his head vigorously. "My head itches, Mama."

Mama looks at his scalp. She scolds, "Stop moving, Jonathan, so I can see your head."

Now the situation moves from bad to worse. Our heroine's eyes widen in great surprise and her face contorts into a horrified grimace.

Our bedraggled protagonist explains the delicate situation to Jennifer, a friend who is staying with the Kays because her house is under ice and a fallen tree. Quickly our heroine bravely slides over ice, around downed trees, and under loose power wires to get to the hospital.

She scratches her head and prays, "Father God, I know you are more concerned about our character than our comfort—but isn't this carrying things just a little too far?"

Feeling the gentle nudge of the One of Great Compassion, she thinks to herself, Maybe I should count my blessings; that always makes things seem better.

Sliding across the ice-cubed parking lot, Ellie carries her little son into the warm building. The nurse asks her to step into the screening room.

Ellie, dressed fashionably in her red wool coat, answers the inevitable paper work questions until the administrative sergeant finally asks the obvious, "What is your problem today?"

Glancing around and already mortified over this embarrassing family situation, she leans forward, her well-groomed hair brushing the counter. The Sergeant, sensing a highly sensitive answer is forthcoming, leans toward the distraught woman and whispers. "Yes, what's wrong?" he asks, giving her a compassionate smile. "You can tell me."

He strains to hear her barely audible answer. "Lice," she murmurs.

The clerk jumps back in his chair, keeping a safe distance from our infested heroine, and motions for her to stay put.

The sergeant quickly finishes the screening process. "You can sit in the hallway outside of the waiting area by the front door." He points toward the designated place of internment.

Jonathan and his mama wait two minutes in the cold hallway. A nurse appears at the private entrance to the clinic. "Mrs. Kay, will you please follow me? And, uh, can you make sure you're at least ten feet behind me?" The nurse obviously read the lice trivia—they can jump up to ten feet.

Walking through the hall, Ellie sees other clinic staff—hiding behind doorways, and generally keeping a safe distance. She fights the urge to yell, "Unclean! Unclean!"

When the doctor arrives, a strange look crosses his face. Mrs. Kay describes the symptoms and places one minuscule dead critter on the examining tray. She backs up five feet. Then the doctor steps up to the tray and examines the evidence, never touching the infested patients. He doles out enough shampoo for all seven members of the Kay household and Jennifer.

The doctor looks at the distraught woman and as gingerly as possible says, "Mrs. Kay, you also need to wash all your family's bedding, towels, clothing, and coats in hot water." Her head nods downward in a motion of defeat.

With no electricity, this will not be a pleasant task.

As Ellie drives home, she wonders how she'll tell Bob. However unpleasant, she must tell, lest he, too, has lice. He could unknowingly infect people at the squadron shelter. She thinks he's at the weather station. She calls him on her cell phone.

The colonel hears his wife's tense voice. "You need to come home ASAP! Don't panic and DON'T say this word out loud!"

The colonel, surrounded by his subordinates, immediately panics. He reacts to the situation with typical dignity and grace. "WHAT WORD? What in the world is wrong?" He jiggles the phone. "What word can't I say out loud? Tell me what's going on!"

Ellie spells out, "L-I-C-E."

Back home again, Ellie, with Jennifer's help, sets about the task of de-lousing the troops. By the time our celebrities are finished, they have added fourteen additional loads of laundry to the already

enormous pile on the laundry room floor. They also have five kids with squeaky clean, lice-free hair.

But now, back to the opening scene of our incredible, true story. Ellie is baking bread and Bob is cleaning the kitchen. The time? 5:00 A.M. The bread is done and they're going to call it a morning.

Will the Kays get all their tasks completed before the power fails again? Will the lice eggs hatch and reinfest the entire family in seven to ten days? Did the lice jump ten feet and get on the doctor? These questions and more will be answered in our next episode of...Kay Family Living.

Hanging on by a thread and a prayer,
Ellie

God forbid you should ever experience a major crisis like ours. Hopefully, you can skip the joys of ice and lice. However, you can learn the joys of saving for a rainy (or icy) day. You can also learn how your experience will help people in need. With all the disasters going on in our home, I was supremely grateful that I didn't have to wrestle with the question many people had to ask: "Where will we get food? How will we get to the store?" At least there was one area I had under semi-control.

Here's a list of the ways a penny saved can yield a dollar today and a whole lot of peace for anything tomorrow may bring.

Tips on the Benefits of Saving Pennies

A Penny Saved Is a Dollar Earned

Did you know that every penny you save is worth far more than a penny *earned*? Think about it. Every dollar *earned* is subject to state and federal income taxes and social security deductions. So every dollar you can save is worth up to one and a half times as much! For example, the $8,000 I saved our family last year is equal to $11,200 to $13,500 (depending upon your current tax structure). I'd have to get a part-time job earning $12,000 in order to match the amount I saved using coupons. Add to $8,000 the savings for everything in this section from clothing to credit cards—and I save the equivalent of $30,000 a year!

Real Versus Perceived Savings

There's a difference between *real* savings and *perceived* savings. Real savings are what we can save with coupons; it's tangible—something we can put our hands on when we need it. Real savings are extremely beneficial. It shows up on a food cost chart—and in your checkbook and savings account at the end of the month.

Perceived savings, on the other hand, are illusive. It's not truly saving if you go into debt, get off your budget, or spend more than necessary in order to "save."

Compounded Savings

Every penny you save is also a penny you won't pay sales tax on. My lovely red wool coat was purchased from the "end of the season" clearance rack. I saved 50 percent off the retail price and 50 percent in additional sales tax. Some states charge tax on all groceries, so the price we save by pinching pennies saves more pennies on sales tax. You've heard of *compounded interest*? Well, this is called *compounded savings*.

Save on Income Tax

We've mentioned this benefit before. Charitable donations of clothing, household goods, and groceries, when documented, are deductible on personal income tax. There's more on documentation of these donations later in the book. Be sure to check with an accountant each year, because tax laws change often. This is a benefit that benefits others—the gift that keeps on giving.

Save on Stress

Saving money is a natural stress buster. Several years ago, the *Dallas Times Herald* had a piece exploring the reasons why a woman in a fur coat, driving a Mercedes, would use a coupon. The findings? Using coupons and "beating the system" gives people, no matter what their income, a psychological boost. You'll find you feel pumped, too, when you can save a buck.

If you use the money you save to pay off consumer debt, you will lighten financial pressures in your home considerably. The number one cause of marital strife is financial problems. You'll find saving money can lessen marital pressures.

It's Your Choice, Mom

One of the greatest benefits of saving money lies in the freedom it gives young families to have choices. I often hear, "It takes two paychecks to get by" or "We can't make ends meet with just one of us working." There's a difference between a woman who has to work and a woman who chooses to work. It's nice to have the liberty to make that choice, rather than to have no control over the situation.

We'll see the hard facts and figures of moms who work outside the home in a later chapter. The main point I want to make is: A great benefit of saving money is the freedom it gives Mom to make the choice to work outside the home full-time, part-time, or not at all.

> She senses that her gain is good.
> Proverbs 31:18

What if I told you there could be strangers lurking in your home right now? Would you be concerned? Of course you would. Well, the kind of strangers I'm talking about aren't the kind that "case the joint" during an ice storm (ask me about that story sometime!)—seeking what they can take. No, these strangers are conventional, and most of the time they are invited into our homes—to rob us of precious money, time, and energy.

The robber could be—your house! Yes, I said YOUR HOUSE! The single, largest expense in any family budget is shelter. Your home could be draining serious dollars from your bank account in a number of seemingly innocent ways. Let's take a look at a few ways to take back what that bandit is trying to steal and—throw the guy out!

Tips to Saving on Housing

To Rent or to Buy?

Whether you rent or buy, housing tends to be one of *the* largest home budget problems. Too many people these days buy a home they simply cannot afford. They do it for different reasons—usually as a result of some form of pressure. We have peer pressure to "keep up with the Joneses." Or we put pressure on ourselves. "Don't I *deserve* to live in a nicer home?"

It's not necessary for everyone to own a home. We must make our decisions to rent or buy based on our family's needs and our financial ability rather than pressures from without or within. As a general rule, you should try to spend no more than 32 percent of your annual net income on a home. Granted, this is a conservative figure, but we are into savings—and financial freedom.

Bob and I have been in the military our entire married life. We've never lived longer than two years in any one location. Buying a home, in our case, would not be a good "move" (so to speak). The two years we pay into a mortgage would not pay into the principal of the note. The resale value of a home, in a soft market, would not cover the closing costs on another home. Based on the housing market areas in which we've lived, it would have *cost us* big bucks to indulge in the luxury of home ownership. This hasn't been a financially sound option—yet!

In an average real estate market, a family needs to plan on staying in a home a minimum of three to four years in order to break even on their initial investment. Every family is different, and we have many friends who own homes and rent them out when they move to their next assignment. On the other hand, we know *more* friends who own homes as an albatross around their necks—causing them a lot of financial worry and loss. Here are some tips to consider when making your decision to buy or rent a home.

Consider Upkeep, Deductions, and Insurance

The monthly upkeep of a home averages around 10 percent of the monthly payment. Consider this cost before you buy or rent a home. If you are renting a home, ask the landlord what they consider upkeep on the property and what is your responsibility.

If you are considering the purchase of a home, calculate any tax deduction on interest paid as a *reduced* part of your monthly payment. After all, if you're getting a tax break, you can figure it into the bottom line. All these factors contribute to the decision-making process.

When shopping for a home, consider the difference in renter's and homeowner's policies. Secure at least three estimates, and look closely at higher deductibles to reduce costs. All these variables are part of the monthly cost of housing and should be considered carefully in your decision to rent or buy, and *what property* you should rent or buy. Which brings us to our next point.

Life Down Under

There may be a millionaire living in your neighborhood and many more in your town. You wouldn't know they're millionaires—but they are. They are usually in their fifties, sixties, or seventies. They're farmers, teachers, accountants, insurance salesmen, homemakers, and a variety of professionals. They all have one thing in common: For most of their lives—*they spent less than they made.* (And 85 percent of these millionaires use coupons.) It's pretty simple, isn't it? Not really. It's hard to live beneath our means when we face the pressure to have more, do more, and want more.

We need to make sure the housing we live in is *beneath* our means, not just *within* our means. We can put ourselves in a position to save for that dream home at a later time. Or we might sacrifice the dream home in order to have a healthy investment and savings plan. In order to exercise any of these options, you'll need to live beneath your means.

In living within or beneath our means, we must consider purchasing a home only if the total payments of the mortgage, insurance, taxes, and upkeep do not exceed 40 percent of the net family income. Otherwise, we won't own a home—it will own us! Let's look at an example of what living beneath your means can do for your finances.

Don't Borrow to Borrow

"Mama, can I have a new bike?"

"Sure, Bethany, but we can't buy it today."

"Why not? They have this nice one in the store and it's for sale."

"We'll have to save the money, and you can earn some of it, too."

"Can't you just write a check?"

"No, Bunny, we don't have it in our budget."

"Well, there's still checks in the checkbook!"

Many American's share my daughter's "checks in the checkbook" philosophy. We think if we can get credit, then we "have" the money. What we "have" is more debt—and a deeper hole.

When it comes to the purchase of a home never finance a second mortgage for the down payment of the home. Never get cash from a credit card advance or a personal line of credit for a down payment on a home. If you have to do any of these things in order to buy the house, then you can't afford it.

Newer Isn't Necessarily Better

Growing up in the United States, we considered an "old" home any-thing over fifty years old—then we went to Europe. Fifty years old is "new" to cultures with thousands of years of history. An "old" home in that part of the world is 300 years old!

When it comes to housing, consider the purchase of an older home that you can improve. (An American old home, not a European old home.) If you put in your own labor and ask your neighborhood handy-man for help, you can increase the value of your home. Older homes oftentimes have better construction, come with more land, and give you more house than you'd be able to afford otherwise.

Where in the World Is Carmen Sandiego?

My children love the PBS show where they answer geography ques-tions to find the ever illusive Carmen Sandiego. Likewise, you'll need to ask questions about a home before you buy. The first and most important element in a home is its location. You may find the buy of the century, but if it's located next to the county dump—what's the point?

Let's say you buy a "fixer-upper" home for $60,000 and put $50,000 worth of renovation into it. The neighborhood homes are worth $75,000. More than likely, you'll never recoup your investment when you decide to sell. You should purchase neither the most expensive nor the least expensive home on the block.

During your look about with the Realtor, do your exercises—bend and stretch. Look over and under everything from the roof to the founda-tion for problems. Once you're quite serious about a house, if it's an older home, hire a building inspector who specializes in older homes. He can advise you of any problem areas, give you an idea of costs to repair these problems, and refer you to reputable contractors.

In handyman specials, avoid homes that have already been remod-eled. While it's fine to tear out original tile and fixtures—it's harder to remove the so-called "improvements" of the previous handyman. Often the plastic cabinets and green shag carpeting you must replace now were part of the price you paid for "improvements" to the home when you bought it.

Mortgage Savings and Penalties

Most of the mortgages available today are written as thirty-year loans. If you must buy this kind of mortgage to afford your home, make sure you get one that does not penalize you for making extra payments in an effort to "buy down." *Buying down* the mortgage simply means the homeowner makes extra payments as financial circumstances improve and as inflation reduces the overall value of the mortgage. The mortgage is paid off early—and big bucks are saved.

It makes sense to pay off your mortgage early—it's a great investment. Most full-time investors do not make 9 percent on their investments. Yet paying down a mortgage will yield that—and more, even after you consider the lost income tax advantage on that mortgage. The exception to this rule would be the mortgage with a low interest rate, of 5 percent or less. That family would do better investing their surplus in an investment plan yielding 6 percent or more.

I'll give you an example. Let's say you buy a $75,000 home at 10 percent interest with a thirty-year mortgage. The first year you'll pay $8,000 on the mortgage. Only $416 will go toward the principal. Let's say you follow your payment plan and don't attempt to buy down the mortgage. You won't pay more on the principal than the interest until *after the twenty-fourth year* of the loan. By the time you've made payments for thirty years, you've paid over $236,000 for your home. The amazing fact is— $161,000 of those payments were made on the interest!

In the above case, the mortgage payment is around $658. If this family rounded up their payment to $700 per month, they'd pay off the loan in only twenty-two years instead of thirty. In the process, they'd save almost $48,000 in interest! The more this family pays, the better the savings and investment. It pays to pay early—as early as you can!

My Daddy Took My T-Bird Away

Tips to Saving on Transportation

January 11, 1998

Dear Friends,

Phone call. Friend in need. "Why don't you come stay with us?" I hear myself saying. No problem. Add two more adults, a child, and a dog to our home. I only hope Dannie the wonder dog (Jennifer's fragrant pal) gets along with Maggie, the golden retriever puppy.

We'll put the family of three on the hide-a-bed in the living room and on the love seat. They are really a nice family, upset at being displaced from their home. Diane, Jaime, and Katie are their names, and I'm just happy we have the room to offer them. I could tell it was very difficult for them to accept our hospitality. As a matter of fact, Jaime was going to sleep in the unheated house (while it's twenty below zero outside) and just bring his wife and child over to our house. He's the kind of guy who thinks about his family before he thinks about himself. He wanted them warm— and he didn't want to impose.

We finally convinced them to stay a couple of days. Diane cried on the phone when she accepted our offer. We have so much and we're offering so little.

Bob is still working around the clock. I'm exhausted. I'm so glad Jennifer is staying here. If it weren't for her, around

> 8:30 this evening, I would have called 9-1-1 and asked them to come bathe Joshua. Thankfully, Jennifer did it.
>
> Love,
> Ellie
>
> P.S. At least the lice are gone—we hope. (Maybe they froze to death?)

Living through that ice storm made me long for the days when I didn't have the responsibility of a large family. While the weather was a frozen wasteland outside and the Kay Circus was on parade inside, I spent a lot of time daydreaming about my teenage years, when life was carefree.

Back then I drove a Datsun B210 I bought for $950 in 1978. When I said I paid for it—that's exactly what I mean. I saved my paycheck from a part-time job, baby-sitting, and industry money (see chapter 17). It ran well, and my girlfriends and I had lots of fun in it.

From the time I was sixteen, I also paid for my gas, insurance, and maintenance on my car. My dad was an excellent mechanic, and this fact helped this little girl out a lot! I learned from an early age that buying used is oftentimes buying best when it comes to cars—and many other goods. Let's see what *little* tips will help save *big* bucks on transportation.

Tips to Saving on Transportation

Why Buy?

One of the first things we need to ask ourselves before we buy any car is—why? Are you tired of your present car? Can the car you have be repaired without major expense? How many miles do you have left on your present car? If you have a loan, how much do you still owe the bank on it? Do you really *need* a new car? Or is it just a big *want*? The new-car bug is a contagious disease in our country today, and when it bites you, it'll seem like your old car is falling apart. The same questions apply to the genuine need for a second car.

The least expensive car you can own is usually the "paid for" car you're driving right now.

The average depreciation of a new car during the first year can be up to 31 percent of the price you paid for it. Incredible! With most new cars, you lose $5,000 as soon as you drive it off the showroom floor. Let someone else own it for that expensive year! Consider the purchase of a late model, low-mileage, mechanically sound, and well-maintained used car.

If at all possible, try to talk to the previous owner of the used car before you buy it—most of these folks will be honest. Be leery of repainted portions of the car—it usually indicates an accident. Look carefully under the car for rust. Once a car starts to rust, there's no turning back. Avoid buying a car from anyone who smokes. Cigarette smoke damages seals, glue, and upholstery. You may be willing to accept *minor*, not major, repairs on a vehicle if it will substantially reduce the price. Be prepared to pay for these repairs, and add them to the cost of the car.

Negotiate for a 100 percent short-term guarantee if possible from the seller (at least one week). This guarantee should apply to dealers and individuals. When you drive the car for the first week, you'll find 90 percent of the problems you bought.

Make a Mechanic Your Friend

Take the car to a reliable and trustworthy mechanic—and pay him to look it over. By the way, the best time to find a mechanic is *before* you need one. Ask your friends, neighbors, or co-workers for a reference. A mechanic's reputation—either good or bad—usually follows him closely.

You'll need a friendly mechanic as your advisor *and* to service your present car. It's always a good idea to be nice to your tool guy. Bake him some snickerdoodle cookies, and don't forget the milk.

Blue Book

Since I was fifteen years old, I've been around the automobile industry. My neighbor, Mr. Bailey, owned a Lincoln/Mercury dealership, and they needed a file clerk/receptionist. I worked every summer, weekends, and after school.

Being around the car lot showed me that those stories you've heard about used-car salesmen can be true. Oh sure, there were nice guys in the business—like Mr. Bailey. These exceptions are the guys we've purchased cars from. One of our favorite dealerships is Berry Chrysler/Plymouth in Corsicana, Texas. They've garnered numerous customer service awards. Their business is spotless and has a wonderful play area for the munchkins. Folks come from as far away as Houston and Dallas to buy their cars in this small town.

I've been around enough dealerships throughout the years to know that once you find an honest salesman—theirs is a friendship worth having!

A trustworthy resource found in most car dealerships is the handy-dandy blue book. This is the book your bank officer also keeps handy. It lists the wholesale and retail value of a used car. The price is affected by mileage, wear and tear on the vehicle, and mechanical reliability—among other factors. You can also check the blue book value on the Internet at www.edmonds.com.

It's *better* to secure a loan from your personal bank—negotiating and shopping for the best price. Know the blue book value of the vehicle and negotiate with the dealership as if you were a cash buyer—you won't be using their banks anyway. Try to never pay more than $100 over the wholesale value.

Trade-Ins

Try to sell your current car privately and don't trade it in. Detail it yourself—washing and waxing it to a glorious shine. As you clean and scrub, think of all the extra money you'll make by this minimum effort—it's surprising! Put an ad in your local paper, and another one up on the bulletin board at work, and tell your friends you're selling your car.

If you trade in your vehicle to a car dealership, you'll get significantly less for it. It doesn't matter how much the salesman "says" he's giving you on the trade. They'll often inflate the value of the trade, then figure the inflated amount in the negotiated price on the vehicle you purchase. It's not illegal, it's just a card shuffle—to make you buy the vehicle.

For example, let's say the sticker price on the new car is $21,500. The blue book value on your used car is $7,000. The dealership says they'll give you $7,500 on your trade. You're ecstatic. Then you negotiate on the sticker price of the car and end up paying $21,000 less your trade, for a total of $13,500.

If you got the normal trade-in value on the car of around $5,500—you could still pay around $13,500 for the car. The sales manager would allow more bargaining room on the sticker price if they had less cash invested in your trade. The difference is—you'd get a $500 discount with a $7,500 trade, and a $3,000 discount with a $5,500 trade. You're better off selling your car on your own and negotiating on the $21,500 sticker price as a cash buyer with no trade. The only exception would be to negotiate the value of the new car separately from the value of the trade-in.

When You Need New

Let's say your old, rich Uncle Harry died and left you as his heir. The only stipulation is you *must* buy a new car in order to collect the millions waiting in the bank. This is about the only reason that you'd *need* to buy a new car. Most people just desperately *want* a new car.

If you must buy new, then try to avoid buying the newest, latest, greatest model—as soon as it comes out. Instead, buy an end-of-the-year clearance model, a demonstrator model, or a rental car. December and January are the best times to get these bargains because that's when dealerships experience their lowest annual sales. Buy a cheaper model of the same vehicle, rather than the luxury model. Buy the smallest car that will still fit your needs.

Leasing a Car

The only way to spend more on a car than buying it new is to lease a vehicle. Leasing a car is the most expensive means of driving a vehicle. The only exception is if you use it for business, anticipate extremely high mileage, and there's a substantial tax savings offered.

If the only way you can drive the car you want is to lease it, then pass on it. There's a less expensive car for you that will still meet your needs.

Alternative Transportation

Since transportation is the moving of goods or persons from one place to another, consider alternative forms of transportation. Some towns we've been assigned to are very small. *How small are they?* I'm glad you asked. They are so small that we can get by with one car. In these past assignments, Bob got rides to work or rode his bike. Yes, it was inconvenient at times—but it fit our budget and eliminated the financial stress of another vehicle.

Car pools, buses, and public transportation facilities are all ways to get your person from one place to another. Even if your alternative transportation is only seasonal, it may help to reassess your genuine need for a vehicle.

Some friends of ours in California, the Rodgers, recently bought an alternate form of transportation, a motorcycle. He's a paramedic fireman and she's a Christian school teacher—not your typical bikers. While leather is not normally Jeanette's "thing," she says it's opened doors to ministry and brought many new friends into her life. It also gives her an excuse for bad-hair days.

Bonus Tip—Saving on Daily Car Expenses

Gas Mileage. To save on gas, try these tips:

• Remove unnecessary weight from the trunk.
• Avoid quick starts—leave these to teenage boys. Drive smoothly and steadily.
• Check the air in your tires regularly; the wrong amount of air wastes fuel and accelerates tire wear.
• Make sure your wheels are properly aligned and balanced.
• You lose four miles per gallon (mpg) by running the air conditioner, and the same amount by having the windows open on the highway (due to wind drag).
• Lose that fifteen pounds you've been putting off losing—you'll save five mpg per month!
• Buy lower-octane-ievel gas—premium gas is only recommended for 10 percent of the cars manufactured today. The rest of us have vehicles that don't need this expensive gas. Also, 10 percent of the pumps marked high octane, or premium, do not actually contain the higher-quality gas. Some states have random testing of octane levels and others do not—so you may not get what you're paying for!
• Get a tune-up, change your oil, and you'll save 15 percent a year on gas mileage.
• Combine errands—instead of running errands several days a week, combine and run all of them on the same day.
• Ride with others in car pools to work, parties, school, errands, the gym, the library, or wherever you and a friend want to go together.
• Buy gasoline at a discount service station and pump your own.
• Walk whenever possible; the best way to save gas is to not use it at all.
• Drive within the speed limit.
• Splurge on quality motor oil; it extends the life of the motor and increases mpg.

Money Wasters

Tips to Cutting the Insurance Fat

W hen I was in the insurance business, I came across some incredible true-life accounts. I could write a book on all our bizarre
cases, but I'll tell you my favorite story. There was a woman and her family who were living in temporary military housing for three months. Her
husband was going through some kind of school, and she and their four
kids didn't want to be separated from him, so they came along. Since this
family didn't have access to a washer and dryer, some generous friends,
Tom and Karen Warren, offered the use of their washer and dryer while
they were working.

The mom of four got a combination to the Warrens' garage door
opener and did her laundry while Tom and Karen worked. Twice a week,
for twelve weeks, the busy mom drove to the Warren home, entered the
combination on the garage door, drove inside the garage, and closed the
door again. She was a creature of habit. Finally the time came to move to
the new assignment—the husband's classes were over.

The night before they left town, the husband packed and prepared the
minivan for the 1,800-mile journey. The mom decided to do one last load
of laundry. While the husband went back to the base to get his orders for
the trip, she went over to the Warren home. The maid was there cleaning,
so the garage door was already open. Creature of habit that she was, she
drove into the garage as usual. Well, not quite.

There was a tremendous CRASH, and glass went flying everywhere as the entire house shook. The maid ran out to the garage. To her amazement, she saw a woman with four kids who had just driven a minivan into the garage door opening *with a travel carrier on top.* The woman's *liability* insurance covered the cost of the Warrens' new garage door—to the tune of $10,000. *Collision* coverage repaired the damages to the minivan. *Medical* insurance covered the evaluation of the frazzled mom.

The medical findings came to a unanimous conclusion: *She's a half-wit.*

Yeah, and I used to be in the insurance business.

In my experience in this business, I noticed two common reactions after an accident. Whether people were involved in a minor fender bender or a totaled vehicle, there was always the universal feeling: What a waste! The second reaction: This really could have been avoided. I heard a lot of "if only's."

Most people (whether they were at fault or not) tend to blame others for their accidents. The insurance business hasn't changed that much: It's still a waste to have "accidents." Especially when *buying* insurance, you don't want to feel as if you're wasting money on either too much insurance or the wrong kind of policy. You don't have to claim "no fault" if you're paying too much in premiums.

The following tips are easy, painless ways to trim the insurance fat. They'll help you spend less money while making sure you have adequate coverage. You don't want to one day say, *"If only* I had read the insurance tips in *Shop, Save, and Share*—I would have known I shouldn't drive into a garage with a travel carrier attached. Now I've got to pay for a new garage door—what a waste."

Tips to Cutting the Insurance Fat

Why Insurance?

In order to save money in this area, we need to define and establish the purpose of insurance. Unfortunately, many families are misled in this area—they're sold a Rolls Royce, when a Ford will do just as well. Insurance is a supplementary provision for the family. It's not complete protection, and it's not a profit-making tool. An insurance plan is not designed as a savings account. It is not for retirement. These are costly mistakes made by the uninformed.

Don't let someone tell you how much insurance you'll need in the event of a catastrophe. They'll tell you how much you'll have to put away for each of your children's college, to provide for your spouse, to pay off every loan you have, to let your loved ones live off the interest of the principal. The guilt trip gets bigger and bigger as the agent's commission gets bigger and bigger.

I'm *not* saying insurance agents are out to get you. I *am* saying that overspending in the area of insurance can put a family into debt. This is when insurance becomes a liability rather than an asset.

Life Insurance

There are many kinds of life insurance plans on the market. You almost need to go to school to understand them—or so it seems. Basically, life insurance can be divided into two categories: term and permanent. The chart on the next page shows the difference between the policies available today.

The basic principle to remember in life insurance is to purchase insurance for *provision* and not *investment.* Therefore, term insurance is cheaper and more affordable. However, you need to evaluate your family's needs and make your decision accordingly. You want your family to be provided for in the event of your death—not benefit from your death.

Remember, the need for insurance diminishes the older you get. Term insurance is still available up to the age of sixty-five or seventy. However, a seventy-year-old shouldn't have the dependents and the debt of a thirty-year-old and will, therefore, require less life insurance.

If you currently have whole life, your reliable agent should reevaluate your program. You may want to convert it to term or borrow the cash reserve and invest it in a program with a higher interest rate. For insurance quotes call Select Quote at 1-800-343-1985 or Quotesmith at 1-800-431-1147.

I'd like to say a word here about life insurance on children. If the purpose of life insurance is to *provide* and not *invest,* then why do we need life insurance on children? Some misguided parents have life insurance programs on their children as investment programs for college—this is not a financially wise decision! Life insurance on children should cover the funeral expenses. They should not be used to pay off debt or for investment purposes. We should not financially benefit from the death of our children. While children are our greatest assets, they're not financial assets—life insurance is designed to protect against the loss of financial assets.

Figure 5

Everything You Wanted to Know About Life Insurance

TYPE OF INSURANCE	ADVANTAGES	DISADVANTAGES
Level Term	Level payments over specific period, usually 5, 10, 15 or 20 years; may be convertible to a permanent policy.	More expensive than ART in early years; less expensive in later years.
Whole Life (permanent)	Fixed premiums; cash value you can borrow against; possible dividends; tax-deferred earnings; guaranteed death benefits.	Initially higher premium than term insurance; little flexibility in premium payments.
Universal Life (permanent)	Flexible premiums; tax-deferred earning on cash value; access funds; different options allow cash buildup or insurance protection.	If interest rates fall, low cash value buildup may cause policy to lapse unless you add money.
Variable Life (permanent)	Fixed, level premiums; guaranteed death benefit; choice of investment options.	Premiums start low but rise with each new term; nothing back if you outlive contract.
Annual Renewable Term (ART)	Most coverage for the least money; protection in increments of one year; can renew yearly up to specified age (usually 70); may be convertible to permanent policy.	Potentially higher earnings than other cash value policies but also greater risk.
Variable Universal Life (permanent)	Similar to variable life but with flexible payments. You select the investment vehicle that generates your cash value growth (stocks, bonds, etc.).	

Health Insurance

The best and least expensive medical insurance you can have is probably the free plan your employer provides. This is usually a group policy offering group rates for dependents as well. Check into the monthly fees and coverage for a competitive price. Some group rates may require that you buy their life insurance policy and may add administrative fees per person. Be sure you are getting the *total* costs so you can comparison shop. After all, we want to compare oranges with oranges, not oranges with apples.

We need to ask ourselves the same question for medical insurance that we asked for life insurance—Why? Medical insurance should be a provision for major medical expenses. A medical plan is not designed to cover Joshua's trip to the doctor for a runny nose or Daniel's strep throat. A medical plan isn't even designed to reimburse the cost of a plague—like lice! A good health insurance plan should cover 80 percent of the medical bills in the event of a *major illness.*

If you have to buy your own insurance, go to the library first and look at *Bests' Insurance Reports* to find an A-rated company whose specialty is health care. Consider raising your major medical deductible to $1,000—since the majority of the premium goes to cover the first $1,000. Make sure your plan has a no-deductible accident provision. You may also want to find a plan that will pay for a second opinion if surgery is advised.

Never buy two policies on one person—you pay twice, but you can't collect twice! Don't cancel an existing policy until you have new coverage in place; you don't want a gap in your coverage.

An Ounce of Prevention Is Worth a Pound of Cure

Taking care of yourself, exercising regularly, and maintaining a decent weight are the best insurance against medical costs. Get regular checkups and teach your children good health habits. Smoking and excessive drinking are both habits that will cost you plenty in the long run.

Taking care of your home and car in the same way you take care of yourself will also yield big dividends. Check the smoke alarm in your home regularly, and make sure your furnace is operating properly. Maintain your car with regular tune-ups, keep the proper amount of air in the tires, and make sure your wheels are properly aligned and balanced. All these tips help in our daily expenses now and can help avoid the need for pricey insurance later.

Homeowner's Insurance

When I was in the business, I created a program to increase the number of homeowner's policies we wrote. I took all of our automobile policyholders' files and checked them for homeowner's policies. All the clients who used us for auto insurance only were put in a pool. I obtained the renewal dates on their homeowner's policies and asked if I could send them a quote at renewal. The surprising fact was that most people didn't know how much they paid each year for their policy. The original copy of their policy was mailed to the mortgage company, and the customer received a copy. The insurance premiums were paid as part of the mortgage payment upon renewal, and they weren't that concerned.

We increased our business by showing our clients how we could help them reduce their monthly payments with a policy that cost less. Our business flourished. Check your annual premium each year, and ask your agent how you can reduce costs. Many companies offer discounts for nonsmokers, fire prevention devices in the home, and installed burglar alarm systems.

Carry only the coverage you need. Generally speaking, you'll want to carry the Broad form and only up to 90 percent of the value of your home. Don't include the land in this coverage. You can't collect more than this amount should you have a total loss, so there's no need to pay additional premiums.

Be aware of the fact that flood insurance is covered *separately* and is purchased from the government. You usually do not need flood coverage unless you live in a flood plain or your mortgage company requires it. The same applies to earthquakes; they are not covered in a regular homeowner's policy.

Reduce your premium by increasing the deductible to $500, $1,000, or 1 percent of the total amount of coverage. For example, if your house is insured for $80,000, with a 1 percent deductible, your deductible would be $800.

Replacement Value/Personal Articles Riders

Make sure you carry replacement value on your personal property insurance. It only costs a little more, and the additional coverage is well worth it. For example, if your pipes freeze and permanently damage your carpet, you'll be reimbursed the cost of replacing your carpet with the same quality carpet—less your deductible. If you don't carry replacement value, your carpet will be depreciated by the number of years you've owned it. You'll have to pay the depreciated difference and the deductible amount—which won't leave much of a check to cover the damaged carpet.

Buy a special rider to cover items excluded from your policy or covered in limited amounts. For example, I knew a woman (not one of our clients) who had a thief break into her home and steal several pieces of jewelry. She had a diamond ring worth $10,000, and assorted jewelry totaling $5,000 more, for a total of $15,000 in jewelry alone. Her insurance only covered $1,000 on jewelry because she didn't have the pieces itemized. The cost of this additional coverage depends upon the total amount of the rider. Check the price of the coverage, and make an informed decision as to whether you want to take a risk on inadequate coverage or pay the additional premium for the rider. We routinely sent out a letter encouraging our clients to cover these special items against theft, a ring lost in the yard, or an item flushed down the you-know-what by the toddler!

The same applies to guns, computer equipment, antiques, coin collections, and any personal item with a "greater than average" value. It never hurts to check with your insurance agent the next time you take her some milk and cookies.

Tenant Policies

If you are renting or live in government housing, you'll still want coverage on your personal household goods. Shop around for a good tenant's policy to insure the contents of your rented home or apartment. There are usually nonsmoker's discounts available. The same information regarding personal article floaters and replacement value applies to a tenant policy, as well as the deductible amount.

Automobile Insurance

One of the very best tools you have in reducing your automobile insurance costs is to drive the speed limit and drive safely. Each ticket you get and each accident add big surcharge points and additional premiums to the cost of a policy. Consequently, if you were given a ticket unfairly—it pays to fight it. If another person was at fault in an accident, *call the police* to the scene to write a police report. Your motor vehicle record (MVR), or driving record, simply lists an accident—it does not indicate who was at fault, and you will be charged for it on your premium. A police report proves you were not at fault and removes any surcharge points on your policy.

If you have several of these points on your driving record, it could automatically put you into a substandard company within your insurance group. Substandard companies are allowed to charge surcharge points—and much higher than standard rates. Don't switch companies until you find out what kind of company you'll be placed into—it could cost you a lot to switch if you have a less-than-sterling driving record.

Secure estimates from at least three major companies before you purchase automobile insurance. Go for the higher deductibles on comprehensive and collision (at least $200 and $250)—you want to insure big accidents, not fender benders.

Liability is required by most states as part of the state law. Liability insurance pays the other person's property damage and medical bills if *you're* at fault. There is no deductible to pay for the other party's vehicle if you are liable for an accident. If you are responsible for the accident, repairs to your vehicle will fall under the collision portion of your policy and they are subject to a deductible.

Medical coverage is cheap. Personal Injury Protection, or Medical, covers you and every person in your car. It is not subject to a deductible. You should get the maximum amount on medical coverage. The "uninsured motorist" portion of the basic policy package covers your vehicle, medical bills, and property damage should the *other person* be responsible and not insured. Under this provision damage to your vehicle is subject to a deductible, and medical bills are covered without a deductible. The company has the option of suing the person responsible for the accident to recover your deductible and the company's costs in the repair of your vehicle, as well as any medical bills.

Reduce the cost of insurance on your car by buying the right kind of car. Some vehicles are far more expensive to insure than others. Check with your agent before you buy a car. If possible, use the least expensive car to travel to and from work. "For pleasure only" vehicles have the cheapest rating, so use that on your most expensive vehicle.

Ask for the Discounts

Some companies offer discounts to nonsmokers and/or nondrinkers (total abstainers). Other discounts include an anti-theft device discount, a safe driver discount, age 30 to 60 discounts, multicar discounts, and a discount for completing a driver's education course. Certain professions, including the military, are given special discounts. Other companies offer a discount if you carry your homeowner's insurance with them.

Bonus Tip—Insuring Young Drivers

The most expensive age bracket to insure is drivers under the age of twenty-one and males until they are twenty-five. Premiums for males are greater than premiums for females. Why? Statistics show boys are more likely than girls to have a major accident. The solution? Only have girls, or don't let your boys drive until they're over twenty-five.

If this isn't a practical solution, then I'll suggest another. Bob Harper, the agent with whom I worked for several years, routinely gave a "youthful driver talk" as a service to our client's children when they started driving. He's a great agent, the kind you'd like to have as a friend.

He showed teenagers the facts and figures. He vividly portrayed the financial benefits of driving safely. He told them how he had some clients who had to sell the brand-new Mustang they got for graduation, because the insurance premiums were more expensive than the car payments! And all because these drivers didn't drive safely—they got speeding tickets and/or had an accident. Kids may listen to a professional when they won't listen to their parents.

Carefully consider when you'll allow your teenager to get his or her driver's license. Once they have that license, even if they don't have a car to drive, they'll have to be listed *somewhere* on the policy. If the only cars you own are fully covered vehicles, with comprehension and collision, it could double your premiums! In most states, it's the law—all household drivers must be listed on a vehicle policy. You can get into expensive trouble by violating this law.

The best option is to put your teenager as a principal driver on an older vehicle. Preferably one that carries only the basic package—liability insurance, medical, and uninsured motorists. Then abide by the terms of the policy. You'll have a good excuse for not letting them drive the newer car. Consider letting your child pay a portion (or all) of his insurance premium—it's an extra incentive to drive safely.

You Shop Neiman's?— I Shop Garage Sales!

Tips to Garage-Saling Success

My motto is: *I may dress our family from garage sales—but we don't have to look like it!* We don't. As a matter of fact, I was dressing Bethany, our bright and beautiful seven-year-old, for church this morning. She primped over her accessories, trying to decide between the cameo (which I wouldn't let her wear—since it belonged to Great-Grandma Laudeman) and the tiger pin (I got at a garage sale for 10¢). "We" settled on the tiger pin.

As I was pinning it on her, she told me a story. *(Now, where does she get the inclination to tell stories?)* "Mama, the week before the ice storm something happened in Sunday school."

She adjusted the bow on her head (25¢) and pulled her new black tights out of the package (15¢). "One of my best friends, Caitlyn, asked me a question."

I straightened the collar on her black velvet dress ($3). "What did she ask, Bunny?"

Bethany handed me her ruby earrings ($5). "She asked me if we were rich or something because I always wear such beautiful clothes."

I helped put on her full-length, black-and-white plaid, fully-lined wool coat ($6). "What did you tell her, Bethany?"

She looked at me in the mirror, and flashed a dimpled smile. "Why, I said, 'thank you,' of course!"

Her secret was safe with me.

Yes, we may dress from garage sales, but we don't have to look like it!

I wasn't always this way. There was a time in my youth when I'd rather hang upside down from the middle-school flagpole in my underwear than admit I bought anything at a garage sale. Not that my mom did a whole lot of yard-saling. She did some, but she mainly bought things from a discount department store.

In my junior high school, the only thing worse than being a librarian's assistant was being a librarian's assistant who didn't own anything from Neiman Marcus. I was both. The popular girls called this incredibly expensive, high-end department store, "Neiman's."

Sara Humphries was the queen of the name brands, and Dina Worthington (the names have been changed) was her royal princess. They wore *Bobbie Brooks* suits, *Calvin Klein* jeans, and *Dior* blouses. Sara had the first mood ring in elementary school and set styles from then on. Dina wore *Charlie* perfume, and her mother actually let her dye her brown hair blond. They shopped at Casual Corner and Dillard's. Their favorite store was none other than—Neiman's.

When anyone wore something new to school, the first words out of Sara's mouth were, "Where'd ya' get it?"

If you mentioned any store other than the top three (see above) she'd turn up her perfectly formed nose and sniff, "Oh, *really?*"

It wasn't that she said anything *bad* about your clothes—it was the *way* she said it. It was like she was really saying, *Oh? You bought that rag at a lowly store? If it were from Neiman's, it might be cute, but since it's only from a common store it has no value. It doesn't matter that it's new and you look good in it—if it's not a name brand. Life, as you want to know it, will simply not exist if you don't have a few things in your wardrobe from the only store that matters.*

Yes, Sara and Dina had the market on clothes in our junior high school.

And I had a terrible secret.

I needed to keep my secret from Sara—although I think she had her suspicions.

My mom bought most of my clothes at—*Kmart*. Shhh! You can't tell anyone or they might tell Sara and company, and then I might as well head straight for the flagpole.

This may seem silly in retrospect, but there's a part of me that still struggles with touting these brand names. There's nothing wrong with shopping at these stores, and there's certainly nothing wrong with quality. It's just that brand names and expensive stores can become the focus. Some women find value in touting designer names and buying clothes they can't afford. They can't afford to pay cash for these destructive habits, so they use their credit cards to pay homage to peer pressure. They're digging a financial hole deeper and deeper—one that impacts their marriage(s), their families, and their health.

My closet is full of brand name clothing paid for by a dime on the dollar—or less. Still my wardrobe consists of quality clothing to be worn to spouse's functions, receptions, dinners, dances, formals, seminars, and even the local gym!

We need to get past adolescent attitudes that lead to bankruptcy. We have to try to get beyond the idea that buying "the best" means buying the most expensive. When we do, we'll experience a whole new world of financial freedom—and quality clothing.

There's a right way to shop at a garage sale and there's a wrong way. Let's come in from the flagpole and take a look.

Tips to Garage-Saling Success

Leave Them at Home

I know this may seem like a callous first tip, especially coming from a loving mother of five—but forget the kids! You're going garage-saling! You'll leave at o'dark hundred and you need to concentrate. Admittedly, if Bob's gone, I sometimes *have* to take the munchkins—then I teach them the finer points of the art. But, if at all possible, it's best to leave them with a friend or at home.

You want to get an early start before the best bargains are gone—but I put limitations on this early business stuff. I've been conditioned over the last ten years of babies to rise early, so that's not the problem. The problem is, if a garage sale advertises a 7:30 A.M. start—I'm *not* showing up at 5:00 A.M. like some people do! I think that's rude, it's inconsiderate —it's just not nice!

Strategize

You need to develop a plan of action. First of all, think about the things you're looking for in a garage sale and make a list. Categorize your clothing, making a complete inventory. Get the right sizes of the people in your family. If you buy things too small, you're wasting money. Do you need a new bike for Johnny? Could you really use a good snowblower? Determine the items you *need* to buy within the next two to three months and put them on your list.

Get a newspaper with the garage sales listed in it and a good city map. Note the starting times and items advertised in the notices. Prioritize the sales according to the advertised items you need most, and plan your route accordingly. You may want to start in the area with the earliest openings. Visit all the sales in the same area to save time and gas. The sales you visit later in the day are more likely to yield a bargain as the sellers announce, "Make an offer."

If you go with a friend, agree on the same strategy. If you can't agree, then go alone.

You probably won't have the time (or the energy) to hit all the sales, so keep your trips to each house short and sweet. It might be a good idea to take along some coffee and snacks if you're going to be out for several hours.

You Aren't Saving If You Don't Need It!

Unlike grocery shopping, I don't buy things at yard sales that I don't need. In grocery shopping, we can get a good deal on tubes of Desitin and donate them to the Crisis Pregnancy Center. But who wants a half-used package of diapers donated to them from a garage sale?

It isn't saving if you're just shopping. A good garage sale mind-set is: Buy goods you will have to buy anyway. If you find a pair of pantyhose still in the package, in your size, for a quarter—then buy them. Instead of paying $3.00 for them at Wal-Mart, you've just saved $2.75! If you'll never wear those hose because they're two sizes too small—then you've wasted 25¢.

The only exception to this rule is when nonprofit organizations are asking for used clothing. I've purchased quality used clothing at garage sales and donated it to the Mexico Children's Mission Project, since they were soliciting used clothing. I've also bought the same type of merchandise for a family whose house was destroyed by a fire—they needed used clothing.

If It's Broken, Don't Buy It!

People have garage sales for different reasons. Everything on their tables and hanging in their awnings is there for a reason. Sometimes the reason is—it's broken. So if you can't plug it in, put a battery in it, or start it—then don't buy it. It's probably broken. Life is too short to buy things you need to repair—unless you know what you're doing.

I learned this little lesson the hard way when I brought home a cracked can opener purchased for a dollar. Every day for the next three months, family members were filled with frustration over this can opener—because it only worked half the time! We finally got rid of it and used a manual can opener.

We've brought home blow-dryers, typewriters, and radios that people said worked—only to discover, much to my chagrin, that they didn't work. That is wasted money. Unless your garage sale is at a friend's or neighbor's house, don't take their word for it.

On the other hand, if repairs are easy (and minor) then buy it. Once Bethany got a beautifully smocked *Polly Flinder* dress for 15¢—it cost $45 new. It had a tear along the seam that took three minutes to stitch. I'll mend a two-inch seam for $44.85—that's worth my time!

If It's Stained, Leave It

You can afford to be choosy at a garage sale. If it's dirty, you can wash it. If it's stained or you can't tell—then leave it on the table. Last week you were paying full price at a department store! This week you don't have to settle for a pair of jeans with an oil stain on them. There are quality products for sale at garage sales that are in great shape. Look for clothing with the original sales tags still on them and products in their original packaging.

Check the zippers, buttons, and snaps on clothing. Pick and probe gadgets to make sure they work well. Count the accessories to a game to make sure all the pieces are there. Look pottery over carefully for nicks, cracks, and dings. Check the knees on jeans to determine wear and tear. Look at the size on a pair of curtains to be sure you have the right size curtain rod. It's not a bargain to buy $5 curtains when you have to pay $25 for a custom curtain rod in order to hang them!

Can This Marriage Be Saved?

People get rid of new things for all kinds of reasons. I love the *newlywed sales.* They have wedding gifts (they didn't like or cannot yet appreciate) still in boxes. Or they have duplicate toasters, microwaves, and coffee makers.

Regularly, we pick up brand new silver, crystal, and china at newlywed sales and keep them on hand for hospitality gifts, wedding gifts, or even a birthday gift here and there. There's virtually no difference between paying $45 for a silver chafing dish at Service Merchandise and paying $8 for the same piece, still in the box, at a yard sale, except $37.

Estate sales have many of the same bargains, especially on antiques. Check the appliances carefully at these sales, though; they tend to be well worn, older units. But if you know what you're looking for, you can find a diamond among the coal.

If you live near a *university* that has family housing, you can find some great deals at yard sales. At the end of each semester, especially in the month of May, student families sell off household goods they can't take with them. It's worth a peek!

The Price Is Right

We don't want to be like the lady who bargains at a *half-price* garage sale—that's rude, it's inconsiderate, it's just not nice! On the other hand, we don't want to pay a price we don't feel good about. If you bought a pair of glass candlesticks, and you paid $5 for them when you really wanted to only pay about $3, then you don't have a bargain.

Let's say you see a pewter picture frame at a garage sale. It's marked $6, a price higher than you feel comfortable paying. First, you need to determine a price that feels good (about $4). Then you go to the seller and ask, "Will you take less than $6 for the picture frame?" The seller will often quote a price less than the price you were comfortable with. In other words, you may get the pewter frame for $3. If the seller names a price that is still too high, you can state the amount you are willing to pay for it. If they hold to the price they came down to, you can feel good about walking away from it. (You'd feel a lot worse if you spent $6 on a frame you felt was worth only $4.) I would remember it every time I looked at that frame in my home. Unless, of course, it held a picture of my garage-saling buddy, Brenda. She would look at something I was holding and give her standard line: "You gonna *buy* that?"

Two Kinds of Garage Sales

The first kind of garage sale is where *they want to get rid of stuff,* and the second is where they want to make money. In the military, we see a lot of the first kind of garage sale—it's our favorite. They have things priced to sell or even give away. Military families move a lot, and they only have a certain weight allowance. They have to trim the extra fat and get rid of the things they can't use.

I don't like the second kind of garage sale. I don't stay long. Most of the stuff at these sales is overpriced (for a garage sale), and the folks get defensive if you ask them to take less. There are too many good sales out there to waste time on an overpriced garage sale. The irony of these two sales is that the first kind makes more money, in volume, than the second.

Stay on Budget

Garage sales need to be a part of your monthly budget. We usually budget $50 a week. This covers even the major garage sale purchases in the long run. The garage-sale benefit greatly diminishes if you go over budget to "save money." It defeats the purpose of shopping these sales.

If you're one given to impulse buying, leave your checkbook and wallet in the car. While you're walking back to your vehicle to get your money, you'll have time to think about your purchase and decide whether you really need it or not.

Cheap Thrills!

Garage-saling is fun! I go out for two or three hours and come back with $300 worth of merchandise for which I paid $30. Let's see, that's a savings of $270 divided by three hours for a total of $90 per hour. There's a psychological boost involved in the savings game and in seeing how God provides for us in little ways.

Last month I found a precious, handmade country craft with two painted girls holding a real quilt on the clothesline stretched between their hands. It's a quality craft that still had the craft show price on it when I bought it—$30. I paid $3. It's hanging in the hallway. As I work on the computer, I see it adorning my country home. The two girls remind me of my friendship with Brenda and our shared passion for saving.

With the help of garage sales, I can redecorate my home without feeling guilty. I "splurge" on clothes for myself at a garage sale and dress well. In our family, a portion of the money I save each week will go to support a children's orphanage in India, a little boy named Kabuli in Zaire, and some poor children in Mexico. There's a unique compensation found in helping others by saving money. When I choose to get by on less, I have the opportunity to share more.

Bonus Tip: How to Have a Successful Garage Sale

Bob came home from work one day and said, "We have to talk."

I'd seen that look before and I immediately knew. "How long do you have?"

He looked ill. "Two weeks."

I was stunned. "Only two weeks?"

Bob was compassionate as he said, "I'm sorry, Beloved, do you think you can handle it?"

Being the model military wife, I answered, "Yes, just let me have a garage sale first."

Our packers would arrive in two weeks to take us to our new assignment. Usually we have more notice, but in this case—it was a chance for Bob to go from flying a "bug smasher" back to flying a "toy fighter." So we took it. (That's a T-41 to an AT-38 for all you pilot friends.)

Actually, we go through our junk every six months so we don't have a houseful of stuff to sort through when things like this happen. Usually I give away our excess to a good home, but in this case, I needed to lose some moving weight. The garage sale was a huge success. Daniel, then six years old, set up a lemonade and cookie stand.

Sometimes when people walked away without buying any lemonade, he would look at them with big, sad, puppy dog eyes and say forlornly, "Thank you for coming—*anyway*." Many of them turned around, came back, and bought some cookies. He made $15!

Four-year-old Philip preferred the direct approach. He had all the makings of a high-pressure salesman.

One man, looking for tools, came up the driveway.

Philip asked, "Do you want to buy them some toys?"

The man scratched his neck and replied, "Not today."

Philip planted his feet wide apart, put his hands on his hips, and looked up at him. "Don't you have kids?"

Somewhat puzzled, the guy met Philip's stare. "Yeah, I have kids." He wasn't used to the Spanish Inquisition—especially from a four-year-old.

The salesman in the little boy went in for the kill. "Then why don't you want to buy some toys? Don't you love your kids? Are they bad children or something? Why wouldn't you want to buy them some toys?"

The man bought a socket wrench—and a toy truck.

Here are some tips to a successful garage sale. Use them as a checklist and handy guide to a profitable sale.

Collect. Throughout the year, throw stuff in a big box marked "Garage Sale." You'll be amazed at how much you can collect. Throwing this stuff in the garage sale box also helps relieve clutter—thereby relieving stress. Once you see how much junk you have, you'll know whether you have enough for a garage sale, or whether you need to buddy up your sale with a neighbor or friend.

Locate. Choose your location carefully. The ideal place to have a garage sale is in a neighborhood where these sales are common. If you live in an out-of-the-way or hard-to-find location, you probably won't have a successful sale. Combine sales at a better location—a family member's or a friend's house.

Advertise. If you live in an area where garage sales are common, you won't need to advertise—a good sign will suffice. Otherwise, take out a small ad in the local newspaper or thrifty nickel. Buddy up this expense with a neighbor having a sale the same weekend. You'll bring her business and vice versa. You won't be competition; you'll complement each other's sales. People want to hit two or three garage sales in one stop!

The sign. Make an attractive sign that is legible and catches the eye. Use a red or blue permanent marker on a white poster board and attach a balloon to the sign. Yours will stand out among common signs, and folks are more likely to remember your address. Have a sign at high-traffic areas in your neighborhood, at each end of your street, and in front of your house—each with a balloon attached. Folks will know they've arrived at a good sale!

Legalities. If your city or housing area requires a garage sale permit in order to conduct a sale, then apply for one. There is usually a very small fee, if any. Some cities just require a completed registration form. You don't want the garage sale police to break up your nice money-making party!

Price It. Mark everything ahead of time and categorize your wares as much as possible. Make sure the prices are clearly visible. If you're having your sale with a friend, use different colored price stickers for each family's goods to keep the money straight. These round stickers are available at any discount store and are worth the investment. Don't throw everything out in the yard without marking anything.

If you don't price your stuff, you require people to ask how much every item costs. They'll either get tired of asking and leave, or they'll buy less. If you take the time to mark your prices, you'll have a far more successful sale than you would if you're not prepared.

Generally speaking, you should mark things from 10 percent to 50 percent of the original price of the item, depending on its condition. People expect to negotiate at a yard sale, so be prepared. Usually there's not as much negotiation at the beginning of the day as there is at the end.

If you don't feel comfortable selling the item at a lower price, then hold firm on your price and ask the person to come back later in the day if he still wants to negotiate. Just as you have to feel good about the price you pay at someone else's garage sale, you have to feel good about the price you get at yours.

Cash. Have enough change on hand to get started. You should have $20 in coins and $20 in one-dollar bills. Get a good container for your money, and don't leave it unattended. Every $50 or so, take the bigger bills into a safe place in the house.

Unless you know the person, don't ever take a check. I know some friends who sold a set of bunk beds for $200 and helped the folks load them on the truck. The check bounced!

Hold it. Don't hold items for people—unless they've already paid for them. The most sincere-looking person may not come back, and you've lost the day's potential to sell it. Experienced garage-salers know they can't expect sellers to hold items.

If the person has paid for a large item, and wants to come back at a later time to pick it up, put a "Sold" sign on it and leave it in the yard. It will continue to attract customers to the other great bargains you have at your sale.

Clean it. You'll get twice the money if you clean it. You don't have to go crazy pressing and washing and dry cleaning everything. Just give your stuff a basic cleaning. Run heavy plastic toys through the dishwasher, put products in their original boxes, hang up as many clothes as you can. I've heard of some folks who shop other garage sales, clean and repair the stuff, and sell it for two to three times as much at their own sales. That's not a garage sale—that's a business!

Market. Just as grocery and department stores use marketing strategies to sell their goods you, too, should think about your marketing plan. Big items, like furniture and bikes, draw people to the sale. Put these items nearest the road in a visible place.

Categorize the sizes of your clothing. Place all similar sizes together, and hang up items that are normally hung. Group similar items together. A cardboard box full of tangled children's plastic hangers is junk. On the other hand, those same plastic hangers tied neatly together in small bundles will bring $1.00. Rearrange your stuff on the tables throughout the day, as previous buyers mess up your marketing strategies.

On the more expensive items, you might want to cut a copy of the item from a sale circular or catalog—with the original price noted. It reminds your customers of the worth of these goods and helps to move them off your lawn!

Expand. You may want to consider broadening your sale a little. If local ordinances permit, you may want to do what Daniel did. Let your children have a lemonade stand, cookie sale, or hot chocolate and coffee stand. In the morning, the hot drinks will go well, and midmorning the cookies will start moving.

Be sure the child is responsible enough to handle money. It's a wonderful opportunity to teach children financial principles. Make sure they have a money box, adequate change, extra cups and napkins, and an ample supply of product on hand. Put two to three cookies in plastic bags. Set up a trash can by the stand for empties. One of our regular stops in the Fort Drum garage sales was a perpetual, weekly sale with hot chocolate and Samoan donuts—greasy and fattening, but oh, so good.

If one child helps another in marketing, they should get a share in the profits. Even though Philip's hard-sell approach was not the best, he made a little money at Daniel's lemonade stand as well—for pushing the benefits of taking home cookies to your children.

I hope you got some good tips from this section. If you didn't, as Daniel would say, "Well, thanks for coming, anyway!"

Hey, Ellie, are you gonna buy that?

Dressing in Style — For a Song

Tips to Dressing for Less

Bethany, or "Bunny," as we call her, is enamored with the stage. Ever since she was an infant, she's loved making people smile. As a baby, all we had to do was look at her and she'd coo and dimple up—melting the coldest of hearts. I don't know where the child gets it.

If she's not making up her own songs, she's singing Sunday school favorites. Bunny's artistic talent usually finds its best outlet among strangers. When she was four years old, we thought we'd find an outlet for the creative angst within this child. We couldn't find a choir she was old enough to join, so we settled on dance classes. We were getting a little leery of impromptu concertos in the supermarket line.

Bethany loved her ballet class and tried hard to do well. In December she was fitted for her spring recital costume, and she was so excited. I took her with me on a rare trip to the mall, found her tights, and proceeded to the registers, a Bunny "hopping" behind me. She was also jabbering as she gushed, "Oh, I'm so excited about my recital. Papa says I'm going to be the prettiest and the bestest.

"The costumes have sequins in silver and pink, and they have tutus and lace and shiny leotards. There's one costume for ballet, the one with the tutu, and there's another one for tap. They have the same leotard, but the tap costume has a special sequin skirt. There's even a special headpiece. When I told Papa about the headpiece, he said, 'Oh, Bunny, it's going to look pre-ci-ous on your whittle golden head.' But I can't wait for the recital. I'm so excited. I think I like the outfit for tap better than the other for ballet and, *blah, blah, blah....*"

I must admit, sometimes I tune out the Bunny channel. An occasional, "Wow," or even a "That's nice, dear," seems to keep her happy. It gives me a chance to think while she jabbers. *These holiday shoppers look anything but jolly. Who says holiday shopping is fun? They look so serious. They look like the "Who's" in "Whoville" after the Grinch stole their Christmas.*

My reverie was interrupted by the fact that Bethany had stopped talking. This was my cue. "Sure, that's nice dear," was my response, even though I wasn't quite sure what she had just said. I had to act as if the radio was still tuned to the Bunny station.

Bethany knew what she was asking and she got the permission she wanted. So she started performing her ballet *and* tap recital, right there, in the middle of J.C. Penney. We saw the first "shuffle-hop step" to the final plie. Bethany decided the dance, by itself, was a little boring. She thought some musical accompaniment for her dance would be nice.

So, she started to sing very loudly. "OH, I'M SO HAPPY, SO VERY HAPPY!" She put all her heart into her song as she flashed a brilliant little smile. I thought to myself, *What am I supposed to do? Make her stop? Should I tell her these shoppers want to enjoy their boredom—without interruption from a singing Bunny? That would deflate her quicker than putting a Duracel battery in the Energizer bunny. That would crush her and I won't do it!*

Looking around the store, I found her enthusiasm was contagious. The other shoppers were actually enjoying their wait in line—and the performance.

"OH, I'M SO HAPPY, SO VERY HAPPY. I'VE GOT THE LOVE OF JESUS IN MY HEART. Down in my heart. AND I'M SO HAPPY..." I was thinking about Bethany's operetta. *This is one of her favorite Sunday school songs. I wonder if she'll do the regular ending.*

I was about to find out—Bethany got ready for the big finish. "OH, I'VE GOT THE LOVE OF JESUS IN MY—" she paused and held her hands out wide, both palms facing up. "GOT THE LOVE OF JESUS IN MY—" here, she turned in a full circle, raising her hands in the air. "GOT THE LOVE OF JESUS IN MY—H-E-A-R-T." I couldn't believe she could hold that last note as long as she did—but she does have her mother's lungs.

As Bethany took a bow, the audience went wild—they clapped and begged for more. They laughed, they cried, it became a part of them. The formerly weary shoppers were alive again as they regained their holiday spirit. Thanks to a little girl who beamed as she bowed in the spotlight. This wasn't the first time she'd performed. Most likely, it wasn't the last. That's all right. I'd rather have a happy Bunny than a boring line.

I imagine you've waited in a few lines in your time, too. Lines are as normal a part of life as eating or dressing each day. The only thing worse than braving a mega line is waiting through that endless line in order to pay top price for an essential item. You don't have to pay top price for clothes anymore.

You can pay 30 percent to 90 percent less for clothing without sacrificing quality or style. The tips that follow will help you to dress in style—for a song.

Tips to Dressing for Less

New Versus Used Clothing

The most obvious way to save money on clothing is to buy it used. Some people get squeamish about germs or think used clothing is dirty. Well, wash it in 120° water, and you'll get rid of any germs and dirt. Do you take your own sheets to hotels? Do you ever try on clothing at a department store?

Some people like the feel of new. Well, if I walked to my closet now, I couldn't tell you which clothes I'd purchased new and which were acquired used. They look the same. Who hasn't bought a brand new article of clothing that puckered or ran after the first couple of washes? Buying clothing new does not guarantee it will wear well.

There is room for new clothes in a bargain hunter's closet, and I have quite a few. We'll look at buying new after we've finished looking at buying used.

Sowing and Reaping

This may come as a surprise to you—but I don't *conduct* a lot of garage sales. As a matter of fact, I've only had two in the last ten years. "Why?" you ask. I'm glad you asked that question. It's because our family prefers to give stuff away. On some of these, like the Salvation Army, we get a tax deductible receipt. On others, we have the satisfaction of giving our unneeded clothing a good home. It doesn't end there, either.

For some reason, we usually receive more than we give. I used to wonder why that was the case. Do we look like a charity case? Do we appear to be the kind of people who need clothes given to them? Then I realized a vital truth—the reason we receive more than we give has to do with the law of sowing and reaping.

If you sow a turnip seed—you'll harvest a turnip. If you sow a grain of wheat, you'll grow wheat. If you sow generosity and give stuff away—you'll reap the generosity of others. We're living proof. Let's just look at the last six months.

We gave away a big garbage bag full of clothes to the squadron fundraiser and to the Salvation Army. About a month later, we got a garbage bag full of clothes for Jonathan and Joshua—thanks to my friend Edna. There were Ralph Lauren and Bugle Boy brand names—all quality clothing. I also received, thanks to my friend Kelli, a big garbage bag *and a half* of clothes for little old me! There were a couple of suits, tons of pants, dresses, blouses, a warm-up suit, and lots more. The brand names included LizSport, Calvin Klein, and other quality clothing.

Along these same lines is the idea of trading clothing. You might want to consider trading your children's clothing with a friend who has clothing your other child needs.

Always write a thank-you note for the clothes you receive. We keep what we can use and pass along the stuff that won't work. When clothes are given to you, the selection is limited but the price is definitely right!

Thrift Shops Versus Garage Sales

We already went into great detail in the previous chapter about clothes at garage sales. This is the cheapest place you can buy clothing. They are usually half the price of thrift shops.

Although thrift shops may have higher prices than garage sales, they also have a greater selection. Also, most thrift shops have a place to try on clothing, so you can better determine fit and style. Some thrift shops have specials—half-price days or buy one/get one free days, among others. Call ahead of time to find out their specials.

Very often, thrift shops are a fund-raising arm for nonprofit organizations, and volunteers at these shops have special benefits. I volunteer at the Fort Drum thrift shop, where the proceeds go to pay for college scholarships. (I like to take Bethany with me so we can do the mother/daughter thing. It's great.) One of the benefits for volunteers at our thrift shop is a first look at the clothing that comes in. Also, the work we do to maintain the thrift shop requires that we go through the clothes on a regular basis. You wouldn't believe the nice things stuck deep inside those racks. Volunteering forces me to find these things and gives me the time to be thorough.

Consignment Shops

These shops have the greatest selection, but the most expensive prices for used clothing. They are often twice as high as a thrift shop (making them four times as high as a garage sale). Some of their prices on children's clothing are as expensive as new clothing purchased on sale at a retail store. However, their prices on formal attire and business clothing are hard to beat. If you develop a friendship with the store owner, he or she can help you find the kind of clothing you need most.

Before You Shop for New Clothes

Look through your closet and take inventory of your present wardrobe. Some of the clothes that you haven't been getting enough use out of may simply need to be altered, repaired, or dry cleaned—thereby saving you a lot of money over buying something new. When you inventory your wardrobe, make note of the items you need most and their sizes.

Take care of the clothes you have, paying special attention to the care instructions on the label. Teach children to care for and maintain their clothing. Before you store your clothes for the season, make sure they are clean. This prevents permanent stains and ensures their usefulness for the next season. Use Woolite for sweaters and lay them out to dry. Use a coin-operated dry-cleaning machine instead of commercial cleaners to save 75 percent on dry cleaning.

Change out of church clothes or business clothes before lounging around the house to save wear and tear on your most expensive clothes. Consider buying classic, long-lasting clothes rather than fads.

Perhaps the most important decision you can make when it comes to buying new clothes is to never buy on credit. You only dig a deeper hole and create more financial stress.

In Season/Out of Season

If you buy clothing before the season begins or in season, you'll probably *pay* top dollar. If you buy your family's clothes at the end-of-the season clearance sales, you'll *save* top dollar. Buy children's clothing with plenty of growing room for next season. Try to buy quality clothing; check the seams, zippers, buttons, and fabric weight before you buy. Always try to buy machine-washable fabrics for savings on dry cleaning and ironing.

In men's suits, stick with conservative styles and dark colors. Select wool or wool blends to extend the life of the suit and increase the wearing opportunity. Always hang up suits after wear, and air them out before putting them in the closet—it helps to minimize dry-cleaning costs.

My friend Edna buys all her son's clothing at end-of-season sales. She buys quality name brands and pays 33 to 50 percent less on new clothes than the average shopper. Her husband is a dentist. They don't have a great financial need, but her philosophy is simple. "Why spend more, when you can just as easily spend less?" When her son outgrows his clothes, she passes them on to someone who will appreciate them—and I sure do.

Sewing

My mother was a wonderful seamstress, but one thing she couldn't do was teach me to sew. She even sent me to the professionals to see what they could do with me. There was a sewing class offered at my high school for four months. They couldn't do much with me, either. I tackled a pair of saddle-backed jeans and made one leg so wide that two legs could fit into it, while the other leg was so narrow that one skinny leg wouldn't fit into it.

Today, I still don't sew clothes, but I appreciate those who can. I'll sew curtains, quilts, pillows, even bedspreads—anything with straight seams. A lot of money has been saved (thanks to my sewing machine) at our house this way, and also by making repairs on clothing.

You can save from 50 to 60 percent off retail prices by sewing your own clothing. These handmade items cost more than garage sales and thrift shops—but the clothing is new and custom-fitted. The savings are conditional upon finding a good price on fabric and notions. Carefully consider the cost of supplies and your time investment before you commit to a project. With the proper planning, you could have a custom-tailored outfit and the satisfaction of making your own clothes. Just don't ask me for help.

Discount Outlets

There is a trend in America for the discount outlet mall, and you'll find one in every large city and throughout Americana suburbia. Watch these outlets carefully. Just because they are billed as bargain outlets does not mean they are bargain stores. Our family went to a Ralph Lauren Outlet store when we were stationed in California. Yes, the clothing was marked down a significant percentage. I suppose if old Uncle Harry said you had to buy a Polo or lose your inheritance, then this would be the place to shop. Still, I don't see how paying $75 instead of $95 for a casual shirt is saving money. The way I see it, it's *spending* money.

Nevertheless, while we were in the Ralph Lauren Outlet, I couldn't resist trying on a full-length, form-fitting, black-sequined designer dress. (In case you haven't figured it out yet—I like formals.) I came out of the dressing room and asked Bob what he thought.

His eyes were popping out; the question was unnecessary. He leered, "I'd say there's a reason we have so many kids!" He shifted the baby balanced on his hip and asked, "How much?"

Smiling mischievously and turning around to face my husband, I asked, "Beg your pardon?"

He smiled back at me. "*For the dress.* How much for the dress?"

Holding up the price tag I read, "Normally it's $5,432—but the outlet price is only $2,799! Can I have it, huh, huh?"

He shook his head. "Naw, we already have enough kids."

The Genuine Article

When you happen upon a *real* outlet, then you've got it made! These outlets offer values that range from 40 percent to 95 percent off retail prices. Look carefully for damaged zippers, etc., and consider each piece and its price. I've found some truly awesome outlet stores that rival the prices found at garage sales. In Tuscaloosa, Alabama, I gave a seminar and had time to visit the Goody's Clearance Outlet. Most of the things were 75 percent off the lowest ticketed price. Of course, there was a size three hanging next to a size twenty-two, and the entire outlet was the size of a regular Wal-Mart store. In other words, some of these places are tough to "conquer." Undaunted, the pioneer blood that runs through these veins was up for the challenge. It took me three hours. When I left, I'd bought sixty articles of new clothing—or $350 dollars worth—for $52. What a thrill!

Modern-Day Servants

Tips to Saving on Furniture and Appliances

E ven though I've got a little pioneer blood running through these veins of mine, I wouldn't want to live in the pioneer days—I'd miss my dishwasher too much. When you read accounts of nineteenth- and twentieth-century living, you'll notice that even middle-class people employed a servant or two. These domestic employees often boarded in the home and cooked, cleaned dishes and clothes, purchased food daily, and served the family in their daily life. Today, we have servants, too. They are called "appliances." They cook our food (oven, stove, microwave, Crockpot, toaster oven), preserve our food (refrigerator and freezer), prepare our food (mixer, blender, dehydrator, pasta maker, juicer), and dispose of our food (garbage disposal, trash compactor). These servants clean our dishes (dishwasher, Daniel and Philip), clean and dry our clothes (washer and dryer), and clean our house (vacuum cleaner). They take care of our hair (blow-dryers, curlers, and curling irons), pretty up our faces (shavers, makeup mirrors, and electric tweezers), and pamper our bodies (foot massagers—yea!). I'm sure you could add to this list, and I believe you get the point. Appliances are modern-day servants.

These servants make our lives easier on one condition—we take care of them. For example, if a certain limited-brained female puts a pacifier in the oven instead of the cupboard, then preheats the oven (some time later) to 375°, the said oven will not "work" well. Instead, it will make the entire house smell like a rubber factory—in case you've never smelled a rubber factory, you don't want to. A clothes dryer works more efficiently when the absent-mind-ed mama doesn't throw a soiled disposable diaper into it (along with the clean load of wet clothes) for an hour. Yep, that's a clear case of "dryer abuse" that should be reported to the local Appliance Welfare Authority as soon as possible. I've also found, through personal experience, that a curling iron works better on my *hair* than on my *hand* (ouch!), and an electric shaver should never be used in the bathtub (it could be an electrifying experience).

None of these servants earn their keep if they aren't working, so maintenance is important. Servants not only need to work well, they also vary in cost and effectiveness. The following tips are designed to help you find, buy, maintain, and appreciate the domestic servants you keep at home.

Tips to Saving on Furniture and Appliances

Maintain

Ben Franklin said, "Beware of little expenses; a small leak will sink a great ship." It's important to take care of those "little things" in the maintenance of existing units. You could significantly increase the life of the appliance.

"Use the unit within the standards suggested by the manufacturer," the new "servant" says. For example, do not overload washers and dryers. I had a friend who thought the washer looked like it needed more water; it was too full of clothes on the largest load setting. So she added a bucket. It flooded her kitchen and caused damage to the washer. Young wives and new college kids usually learn the hard way that it's not worth saving quarters by cramming the washer with a whole week's worth of laundry. The clothes come out dirty and have to be rewashed.

Before discarding the old furniture or appliance for a new one, get an estimate on a complete overhaul. Or better yet, can you repair or rebuild that couch with a fix-it guide? Can you learn to reupholster and varnish as a new family hobby?

Save for an Icy Day

Some folks save for a rainy day—not in the North Country. To save the most on furniture and appliances, you should prepare for these purchases *before* you need to make them. Set aside an emergency fund with as little as one percent of your monthly income—building up the fund to a healthy amount. When you need a replacement unit, you'll have the cash and won't spend more by using credit.

When it comes to furniture, much of what we think we *need* is simply what we *want*. Evaluate your genuine needs in furniture. Can you re-cover that couch with fabric from a wholesaler? Do you really need bunk beds when the single beds you have are still in great shape?

Remember our old saying? People don't plan to fail with their finances, they just fail to plan—ahead!

Consumer Buying Guide

Go to your library, or consider purchasing a current *Consumer Buying Guide* on the appliance or furniture you need. Rely on their extensive research on the most reliable models. If you are buying used, get back issues of *Consumer Buying Guides* to determine the best values in years past. ProQuest is a research program available on most library computers. They have access to over 1,200 periodicals and journals and make this information readily available. If you know your way around the Internet, you can find consumer information on the information highway.

The *Consumer Buying Guide* will list price ranges, reliability, and other comparisons of different models. If you do your homework before you shop, you'll know what features you need and the prices of the appliance you're shopping for. Attacking the stores with your Consumer Reports information will make you dangerous to the salespeople.

And remember—adding a bucket of water to your washer will make you dangerous to your appliance. Read and *believe* the manufacturer's instructions.

Buying Used Appliances—From Individuals

As with our previous sections, the best bargains on a replacement unit will be found in the used appliance section of your newspaper. Since this is a greater investment than a 50¢ pair of jeans, you'll need to proceed with caution when you purchase a used appliance.

Due to households breaking up or combining, people transferring to different areas, and families who upgrade, you can find a bargain at a garage sale or in the newspaper. If you buy from a garage sale, you'll need to show up early, as these items go fast. Ask the seller how the unit works, and ask for a written receipt with his name, address, and phone number. List the information regarding the condition of the unit on the receipt. If he says it "works just fine," then you might ask him to sign a receipt and guarantee the information he's given.

If the seller won't back up his word, then buyer beware. If he will, then you'll probably want to take the unit home immediately and hook it up. If it does not work, you'll still have time to return to the sale and renegotiate. Before I put on my traveling shoes, I owned a little house in the woods in Texas. I bought a washer and dryer for $100. The woman signed a receipt, and my units worked well for two years. Then I sold them for the same amount, moved from Texas, and the rest is history.

Becky Freeman, that witty writer and fabulous friend, shares about her early marriage: "We bought a washer from our local Laundromat for $25. My mother covered it with contact paper—as if that would camouflage it. It was ugly, but it sure was cheaper and tons more convenient than Laundromat prices."

Buying Used Appliances—From a Store

The next step up from a garage sale is a thrift shop, and there aren't too many that carry major appliances, but it's worth a few phone calls. Shop as much from home as you can, rather than wasting gas traveling from store to store. You may want to try the service repair shops. Call and ask them if they sell reconditioned units.

A used appliance store, or a new appliance store with a used appliance section, can yield great values. Be sure to negotiate on these units. Ask for a warranty from your dealer, and ask for free delivery and setup. They may balk at the latter, but they'll oftentimes throw it in. If they won't, then borrow a pickup truck and do it yourself.

We bought a Maytag washer and dryer for $500 (for the set) from an appliance store with a used section. They were a year old and still had a warranty left on them. The previous owners wanted a couple of extra gadgets on their units and traded these babies in. They lost big time. We gained big time. That was ten years and 5,200 loads ago. The Maytag man came to our house once—when the washer was damaged in a move. We haven't seen him since.

Buying New Appliances

When I was in elementary school, I was quite the young entrepreneur. Even way back then I was thinking about saving money. As a matter of fact, my favorite song was "You'd Better Shop Around" by The Captain and Tenille.

It's still my favorite song—when it comes to lullabies and when it comes to buying new appliances. When it comes to appliance service contracts, you'll probably do best to pass on them. Some contracts duplicate your manufacturer's warranty, and others are usually not cost effective. It's best to take your time and avoid buying under pressure.

Look at discontinued units and last year's models. Consider buying your purchase on a gold card that offers double manufacturer's warranties. Then pay that card off the very next month. Incurring more debt *costs* you money. Avoid the deluxe models—they have too many extra bells and whistles. You don't need them. We bought a small freezer and saved 35 percent by eliminating two unnecessary features. We decided we had enough noise at our house without the new freezer dinging and whistling.

Buying Used Furniture

At a garage sale, these things go fast, so you'll probably want to shop early. If you hear of a friend who is buying a new bedroom set, and you need one for your teenager—consider asking what they want for their old set. Look in the classifieds, and call before you go by anyone's house to view furniture.

It's important to call on these ads with specifics in mind. If you ask the seller the color, size, shape, condition, and guarantee of his furniture—you can read between the lines and save yourself a lot of time, gas, and energy. It's a good idea to do the same thing with thrift shops, consignment stores, and used furniture stores.

Once you're there, sit on it, step on it, look under it, and turn over the cushions. Check for previous repairs, stains, tears, seams falling apart, and overall condition of the piece. Be prepared to transport your own purchases from garage sales and individual homes.

Buying New Furniture

Once again, you need to shop around—town. With your handy-dandy *Consumer Buying Guide*, shop the sales at each furniture store. Compare warranties, delivery charges, and features. Consider mail order houses for furniture. In order to maximize your benefit from mail order houses, visit a furniture store first and select the brands and styles that best meet your needs and your budget. If you know the brand name and model, you can check the mail order houses in the back of women's and home magazines to find the contact for manufacturer direct purchases. Call these people and negotiate on the phone for a good price—be sure the bottom line includes shipping and handling. Compare these prices with what the local stores have to offer.

Look at discontinued pieces of furniture and last year's models. Shop the wholesale stores, and take your time. The more you look and watch the advertisements for sales, the more satisfied you'll be with your purchase. Ask the salesman when the item might go on sale. If you just missed a sale by a couple of weeks, ask the manager for the previous sale price. Oftentimes you "have not because you ask not."

Small Appliances

There was a rhyme from the Depression era that my wonderful great-grandma Laudeman used to tell me when I was a little girl: "Use it up, wear it out, make do—do without." I have the same philosophy—with a '90s attitude. Let's look at each line of this rhyme.

Use it up. Let other people get rid of a toaster because it doesn't fit their color scheme. If it still works well, then use it up. You can buy other folks' rejects (in your color scheme) at a garage sale for one-tenth the price.

Wear it out. This is similar to the above with an exception. In small appliances, you may have to repair a knob or a screw and it will have more life to it. Make sure the thing is really dead before you bury it.

Make do. Okay, you feel deep down in your soul that you can't live without a Black and Decker under-the-cabinet can opener. Those commercials have you convinced! You *need* the extra space on your counters, and it looks so spiffy under the cabinet. Besides all that, you'll look like the beautiful model in the ad if you buy the product. But your present can opener works great, and it's only a year old. Stop coveting and make do.

Do without. There is far more in life that we can do without. Simplify. Do you really need all those little appliances that take up so much room and perform such a limited function? Go to garage sales, and you'll see all the stuff folks can do without. There you can buy your juicer, dehydrator, pasta maker, bagel baker, jerky jerker, taffy puller, and...well, I think you get the idea.

Ask Mom

This is a rather unconventional tip, but why not ask Mom for her rejects? Sometimes other members of our families have that piece of furniture or appliance that we really need sitting in their storage shed. It's gathering dust and corroding for lack of use. It could be ours for the asking.

I've also seen these items, believe it or not, sitting outside by the curb waiting for the trash man. I'm not saying we should start crawling in dumpsters, but bargains are all around us if we have the eyes to see them. Start developing a savings mind-set, and you'll find great deals in the least likely places.

Girls Just Want to Have Fun

Tips to Saving on Entertainment and Travel

She had long red hair, liked to laugh, and wore a plastic Oreo cookie necklace. I played the "burping bedpost"—our nickname for the bassoon, and she played the clarinet. From the first time I saw her sitting in Mr. Pitt's sixth grade band class, I knew she'd be my best friend. Donna Nicholson was not just an average friend, she was a kindred spirit—she still is. Although now she's Donna Thomas, RN, wife of Rob, and mother of three precious girls.

We were good girls. We got mostly As and went to the church youth group together. We even went to a nursing home on Sunday mornings. Donna would sing and I'd sight-read on the piano. We took special requests from the audience, mostly the old hymns. Of course, I couldn't play any song with more than two flats. Most of the special requests had three or more flats or a gazillion sharps. That didn't phase us—we'd wing it. All I can say is—it's a good thing most of our audience was hearing-impaired.

While the rest of the kids went to parties to get rip-roaring drunk, Donna and I made our own fun (even without the alcohol). We'd make an appearance at a party and leave early. We'd go roaring around in my Datsun B210. One of our favorite games was called "Panic Attack." My Datsun had seats in front that instantly fell flat backward at the pull of a lever. We'd drive up to a stoplight next to a middle-aged couple. When I was sure the couple was looking at us—Donna would "drop" in her seat.

She was completely out of their view. I'd give an exaggerated mime of alarm and despair over my fallen friend. Most of the time folks knew we were just having fun—much to our disappointment.

Sometimes, if we were lucky, the *woman* would get concerned. She'd convince her husband that we really needed help. We could only hope he'd ignore his better judgment. If he did get to the point where he started to get out of their car to help, Donna would pop up in her seat. We'd wave at them and drive away.

When we were young, we made our own silly entertainment. And some of us grown-up kids continue that trend. It's not only good for the heart, its good on the budget. Here are a few ways we've found to keep kids and grown-ups alike happily entertained—on a shoestring, of course.

Tips to Saving on Entertainment and Travel

Redefine Entertainment

I can always tell when Bob is reading the Sunday comics. His guffaws echo throughout the house. Indeed, he laughs so loud, the *neighbors* hear him. It gives them something *else* to talk about. He has fun reading the comics and the kids enjoy watching him. They pull up chairs and make microwave popcorn. If the truth be known, this is the real reason we're late to church on Sunday mornings.

When Bob is confronted with his embarrassing guffawing habit, his explanation is straightforward. "It takes so little to keep an idiot happy." Life's simple pleasures *truly* are the best.

Plan Ahead

One of the reasons many families overspend on vacations is because of a failure to plan ahead. Set a budget before you pull out of your driveway. Decide what activities take priority and *stay on budget*. Let everyone in the family contribute their ideas, and decide on a plan that will accommodate as many of the family's interests as possible.

Estimate the cost of meals, gas, and incidentals. Let your family members know about your budget so the tourist traps and unnecessary souvenirs won't tempt them. Give each child a predetermined amount of spending money. Plan your vacations during off-seasons, if possible—

you'll save significantly on everything from hotel rooms to area attractions.

Select vacation areas in your locale. Since we move so much, we try to see everything there is to see within our area. We make day trips to area sites and save the cost of a hotel room. We pack our lunch and have a great time relaxing at a roadside picnic table.

We bring along the comics, the kids pull up chairs, and the guffawing commences.

Dinner and a Movie

Who says we have to go to a full-service restaurant and first-run movie in order to have fun? You can cook a nice meal at home for those out-of-town guests, and you don't have to spend $50-$100 on a meal. If you want to invite several couples, or families, make it a potluck. Pick a theme—like a Mexican Fiesta, or Country Western potluck.

If you just want to get away for a while, pick the bargain matinee or dollar theater and eat dessert afterward. Better yet, go out for ice cream and rent a video for the night. First-run movies will often make it to the video market in as little as nine months. We buy *Movieguide* and monitor their recommendations for younger viewers. This review guide is available for $40 a year, and it's well worth it. Call 1-800-899-6684 or write them at Good News Communications, P.O. Box 190010, Atlanta, Georgia 31119. Or visit them on the net at www.movieguide.christ.com.net. It's easier to turn off a $3 video than it is to walk out on a $40 family night movie at the theater. If you insist on going to the theater, you might want to pass on the sodas and popcorn—I've heard some of that stuff is life-threatening anyway.

If you want to take the family out for dinner, check the local restaurants for specials. Family nights are sometimes offered on Tuesdays or Wednesdays.

For example, a restaurant in our area has a Tuesday night special where kids eat free. There's a limitation of two free kids' meals per one adult meal. Since our two youngest never finish their food, they can easily split a dinner. We feed the whole family a great meal at a full-service restaurant—with ice cream, for around $12—that includes a 20 percent tip! Check out the bargains available, using your yellow pages and phone. You'll not only save on gasoline, you'll save big bucks on dinner, as well.

Save on lunches and dinners by drinking water with your meals. Our family saves anywhere from $7 to $12 on a regular-priced meal by drinking water instead of soda. Consider splitting meals at restaurants that offer large portions. Your wallet *and* your waistline will benefit.

The Library

The local library offers a lot of fun for adults and children. You can borrow videos, books-on-tape, CDs, and audiocassettes, besides the ever-popular books. Many libraries have storytime; they also have special summer camps and may offer lectures.

Computers are popular at libraries, and you can learn your way around the WorldWide Web or research information through their ProQuest programs. Children and teens need supervision for their journey on the Internet, for there are some not-so-nice places on the web that little eyes shouldn't view. Many libraries have "Friends of the Library" book sales that yield great bargains—and you'll have that source of entertainment as a permanent part of your home library!

Games

During our ice storm experience, families in the area learned the lost art of fine game playing. You know all those games the kids get for Christmas and birthday gifts? They may be taking up space on a shelf when they could be a great source of inexpensive entertainment for your family. These games are readily available at most garage sales, too. An added benefit is the communication that is opened up during game playing.

Sports and Exercise

Killing two birds with one stone is one of my favorite pastimes. I like to take a walk and visit with a friend at the same time. It accomplishes two important functions—exercise of the legs and the jaws. Your family may want to pick up a sport as common recreation. Basketball, soccer, baseball, and jogging are all inexpensive and fun sports to participate in as a family. Swimming is one of our favorite sports. That is, as long as Joshua and Jonathan don't take off their swimsuits in the middle of the pool area (again).

Air Travel/Cyberspace

Sometimes business or pleasure or your mother-in-law requires that you travel by air. Purchase your tickets ahead of time. You can save as much as 60 percent off the standard fare by planning ahead.

There are many good resources to getting around the airline's multilevel fare system. One is found on the information highway—which can take you places inexpensively. Try some on-line travel agents, like Travelocity (http://www.travelocity.com), Expedia (http://www.expedia.com), or PreView Travel (http://www.previewtravel.com). You can get fares that conventional travel agencies say don't exist. You might have to book these fares on line. These website services allow you to search for the lowest airfare available to your destination and then research whether the travel restrictions and dates fit your needs. Not even a travel agent can do that!

There are some good books on saving money on airfare, also. One I've read is *The Airline Passenger's Guerrilla Handbook* by George Grown (Blake Publishing Group). See if your library has this or any other books on legal ways to save on air travel. If you travel a lot, join a travel club that will give you a cash rebate of 3 to 5 percent on domestic flights.

Airfare—The Master's Level

The Internet Travel Network (http://www.itn.net) has a low-fare ticker you can activate and keep as a computer screen saver. Bargains will scroll across the screen, alerting you to the latest in airfare savings. A useful source on last-minute travel bargains is Best Fares (http://www.bestfares.com). It is part of the on-line magazine *Best Fares*. There is an annual subscription fee of $59.95 (at press time), but it offers all kinds of incentives and coupons.

Consider buying two round-trip tickets if you must travel during the week and miss the Saturday stay-over savings. Many airlines require that you stay over the weekend to satisfy the cheaper rate. Let's say you have to fly from Dallas to Phoenix. Buy a round-trip ticket from Dallas to Phoenix, and a round-trip ticket from Phoenix to Dallas. On the way to Phoenix you'll use the first leg of your first ticket. On the way back home to Dallas, you'll use the second leg of your second ticket. Throw the other tickets away and save as much as 17.6 percent.

Buy a late night or "red-eye" special for large savings. Show up for an earlier flight and ask the ticket agent *at the gate* if you can fly standby. Bring your coupons and work on them while you wait. If there's an available seat, most airlines will let you take the earlier flight with the discounted ticket. Joining a frequent-flier program is a must for the person who travels a lot. These points are worth about two cents a mile, and remember, a penny saved...

Federal law only allows some airline companies to fly to adjoining states. Check the rates to see if it's cheaper to fly to the next state and then take another flight out on the same airline. You may have to wait for the second flight to your second destination due to federal requirements. It's worth checking into.

Check the paper for discount airline fares. They offer great savings, although the limitations are strictly enforced. There's no flexibility for these kinds of fares, and they're subject to expiration dates.

Alternative Forms of Travel

Flying isn't the only way to get from one place to another. Trains are sometimes a cheaper form of transportation. Check out the fares and schedules. Then there's always the bus; you can meet some interesting people in that form of travel. You'd probably get enough material in just a few short trips to write a book.

Consider carpooling with other families to the same destination. Share the expenses of your vacation when you get there, and you'll be able to enjoy added savings *and* fellowship.

Camping

We've saved the best for last. According to family surveys, the most common denominator in individuals who expressed a satisfying childhood is—camping. The family that plays together stays together, and this is especially true in the great camping adventure. Before you take the big plunge and buy a camper, tent trailer, or motor home, consider renting a camper for a weekend.

However, the least expensive way to camp is tent camping, and it's truly a family bonding experience. Camping saves money on hotel rooms and food. You may want to consider pooling your equipment with other families to save expenses. For the novice, joining an experienced camping family is a must. We learned so many helpful tips while camping with the Parker family on the annual July 4th weekend trip. We forgot the eggs, but they remembered them. We forgot the bait, but they had plenty. We forgot the babysitter, but Grandma Pauline was there. Camping can be a great, relaxing time!

Moneybags

Tips on Savings, Debt, Credit, and Banking

When it comes to money, there are basically two kinds of people—spenders and savers. The savers naturally hoard every penny they can tuck away, and the spenders blow it before the coin can see the inside of a pocket. These personality traits are usually exhibited from an early age. Take a famous saver, for instance—me.

Yes, from the day I was born I was saving someone something. I was due on February 3, and I arrived six weeks early, on December 28—just in time to give my dear old dad another income tax deduction. I've felt like he owed me ever since.

Then I saved my mom a lot of expenses, too. I was the second girl instead of the desired son. I could wear all my sister's clothes—thereby saving her lots of sewing time. I kind of figured she owed me, too. My little brother came along five years later. He was born in June and had no one's hand-me-downs. I figure he owes Mom and Dad. Big time.

My saving tendency grew as I grew. By the time I was in the second grade, I had my first thriving business. I got a great toy from a box of cereal. I tucked it in my hand, and when I shook hands with someone, it buzzed—scaring them in a thrilling way. I convinced all my classmates that this was the greatest adventure since Neil Armstrong walked on the moon. They were impressed; we were studying the great moon walk in our science class.

I charged for handshakes, and I saved my money. It cost a girl 10¢ to get buzzed, and it cost a boy (yuck!) 15¢. I charged extra for the mental suffering involved in touching a boy's hand. I made around $10 in ten weeks—that's a lot of handshakes. Just like my parents taught me, I put $1.00 into the Sunday school offering plate and saved the rest. That was only the beginning.

I took my stash home and showed my parents. They were savers, too, and were pleased. Dad tugged my braid, "Why, you little moneybags." The prophetic nickname stuck.

In third grade, I sold my grandmother's vegetables door to door. I convinced my "abuela" that I could get twice as much for eggplant as the grocery store charged. I sold all our eggplant; there wasn't any left for our family. I hated eggplant. Abuela and I had a 60/40 profit-sharing partnership ratio. I figured she owed me for doing all the hard work—selling. At least she made 40 percent.

By the fourth grade, I'd saved up a pot of money, and my mom wanted a cut. I really wanted to go to Pioneer Girl camp, and she said I'd have to earn half the money myself. Well, twenty-five dollars was my entire nest egg, so I expanded my business to a product I could sell well—chocolate. Mom and Abuela took me to Kmart, where I bought small candy bars for 35¢ and large ones for 50¢. I sold them for 50¢ and 85¢, respectively.

I had a hazelnut flavor, as well as orange, date, and fruit. There was also milk chocolate and dark chocolate. My door-to-door business went pretty well. I think people liked my black braids, toothless grin, and big pearl-and-diamond earrings. That was before I found out reselling chocolate was a crime (in more ways than one). I would never *dream* of selling my chocolate today!

By the time I was in the fifth grade, I'd added another business to my home-based corporation of companies. It was the "critter" business. I was inspired when I went with my mom to Hancock's Fabrics. In the back of the store, they had a special selection of fake fur. The business idea hit me, and I bought a half yard of blue fur and a half yard of orange fur. I also found several packages of plastic eyeballs—medium-size. I funded the start-up costs with money from the handshaking business—which was now in receivership due to an oversaturation of the market by other entrepreneurs.

I made furry critters; the small critters were 45¢, and the large critters were 65¢. You could buy both for an even dollar. Through marketing techniques, I convinced most of the fifth grade class that these critters were an essential part of their emotional well-being. They bought them for themselves, their friends, and their parents. My critters were so popular, they were turning up everywhere. Even in the principal's office. That visit had something to do with operating a multimillion dollar corporation out of a classroom locker. The critter business went underground.

In the sixth grade, I became an inventor. I created all kinds of gadgets from my dad's old refrigerator boxes. He was a building contractor and a thoughtful guy. He brought home all these boxes for us to play with—who needed to buy toys? I invented a vending machine and an automatic puppet show. Alas, none of these proved to be profitable, and I had to sell off the invention business at a loss.

Despite my losses, I maintained the other businesses so well that I was able to pay for half a trip to Spain with my abuela to see my aunts, uncles, and cousins. My parents decided "moneybags" could fund a portion of this trip. A saver just doesn't make those decisions on her own. I guess they figured I owed them.

Like any good businesswoman, I took my setbacks in stride and bounced back with greater vigor in the seventh grade. I was now old enough to baby-sit. I earned a lot of money from these jobs, for I was conscientious about my work. I already knew about supply and demand. If I supplied an outstanding service—I'd be in great demand. Since I was only one person and becoming a popular sitter, I could charge more. That's exactly what I did. I had the highest rates on the block, at $1.50 per hour.

Under the guidance of my mom, I established corporate policies for my clients. They had to book me at least one week in advance or they were charged a penalty. If they canceled within forty-eight hours of the job, they had to pay me for the night's work, since I undoubtedly turned down other jobs to save their place. For party animal parents, I charged $1.75 after 10:00 P.M., $2.00 after 11:00 P.M., $2.50 after midnight, and $3.00 after 1:00 A.M. I'd baby-sit two families at one time, but each had to pay me my regular rate. I enjoyed the double-dipping nights. I had no problem handling larger crowds of kids—an experience that has served me well.

In return for their business, I played with the kids, fed them dinner, bathed them, put them to bed, dispensed ear medicine, changed diapers, fed and burped babies, did acrobatics with the children, took accurate phone messages, cleaned the kitchen after dinner, straightened the house, and picked up the children's toys. Yes, hard work was a hereditary trait in my family. The kids begged for me whenever they needed a baby-sitter. Plus, I usually got a fairly nice tip.

Regular baby-sitting jobs continued to flourish until I was in the ninth grade, when I got a part-time job with my neighbor, Mr. Bailey. He owned a car dealership and asked for me by name because I baby-sat his herd of girls and did a good job. The Baileys were a generous family and good tippers, too!

From the age of fourteen, I worked full time every summer and on weekends for the car dealership. At sixteen, I added a part-time job after school for a spa company, and then for Best Products. I paid for my first car by the time I was fifteen. I bought a new car at eighteen. I paid for my insurance, gas, spending money, clothes, retreats, and camps, and basically anything else I needed (or wanted). I *didn't* pay room and board, but I did my own taxes. I maintained and balanced a checkbook from the age of twelve.

After I did a little growing up, I realized life is a lot sweeter if we don't keep score. I learned that the dollar for every ten that I put in the Sunday school offering plate was the sweetest dollar I made. Besides that, I found that giving into the life of others is an investment in the eternal—souls. I added a new policy to my corporate statutes. You can't outgive God—so don't keep score. I've managed my business affairs and home-making affairs with God's grace—and the mentality of a saver turned giver.

You may not be a "moneybags," but all of us deal with money every day. We either owe money, earn money, spend money, burn money, or save money on a regular basis. Consequently, anything we can do to improve our cash flow (and keep it flowing) is to our advantage to learn. There are some simple tips that will help "moneybags wanna-bes" handle their money more effectively—specifically in the areas of savings, debt, credit, and banking.

Tips on Savings, Debt, Credit, and Banking
The #1 Tip to Save on Credit and Debt

If at all possible—don't borrow.

Borrowing

We should use great caution in borrowing for anything. The best rule for credit is to avoid borrowing on a highly depreciating item (i.e., luxury cars, appliances, furniture, food, vacations, etc.)—a difficult task in today's easy credit and "buy now" society. If you purchase these items with cash, you'll be financially healthy.

Never, ever borrow, or use your credit card, for an impulse item. Use the thirty-day rule. It's a plan I read about way back in 1978, in Larry Burkett's book *Your Finances in Changing Times*. It's still a good rule today. If you think you need the item, wait thirty days. If you still think you need it, and it's available, then consider purchasing the item. If it's not available, you are probably better off without it. You'll be amazed at how effective the thirty-day plan is for debt reduction and financial health.

If you use your credit card for convenience, then pay it off when the bill comes in to avoid interest charges. If you can't pay it off immediately, then cut it up. There are benefits to using credit cards *if* the balance is paid off monthly. For instance, some gold cards offer double the manufacturer's warranty if you use their card.

If you must borrow, shop for the lowest-cost loan you can secure. Make sure the item you're buying will last longer than it takes to pay off the loan. Don't co-sign on a loan unless you are willing and able to pay the debt—*without* repayment from the borrower. Chances are that's what you'll end up doing anyway.

Make sure the benefits of borrowing *far* exceed the cost of the loan. For instance, when we bought our almost new, cherry red customized Suburban, we got an exceptional bargain. We took out a loan for a portion of the vehicle and got a twenty-four-month note from our bank to pay it off quickly (and we paid the debt early). When we drove it off the dealership parking lot, we were offered $3,000 more than what we paid for it. In this case, the Suburban was not a highly depreciable item.

Credit Cards

We've touched on a few applicable principles on credit card buying in the above tips. Let's take credit cards one step further. Call or write Bankcard Holders of America, 524 Branch Drive, Salem, VA 24153. Ask for a list of the credit cards that offer the best rates. There is a small fee for this service, but they can save you lots of money. In this research, find a company that does not require an annual card fee.

When you research the card, you'll find information in compliance with the new Federal Fair Credit and Charge Card Disclosure Act. This law requires all credit card solicitors to provide a uniform table with the following information: (1) annual percentage rate, (2) annual fee, (3) minimum finance charge, (4) grace period, (5) transaction fee, and (6) method used for calculating balance. Even if you pay your cards off at the end of the month, some of these points of information will impact you financially.

For existing credit cards, call the company and ask them for a lower interest rate and if they'll waive the annual fee—or you'll switch cards. You'd be surprised at how many companies will lower their rates to keep your business. It's worth a try.

Consider using your credit card as a means of securing a lower cash price for an item. Ask the manager or store owner if you can receive a 5 percent discount by paying cash instead of using your credit card. Retailers have to pay the bank a fee when a credit card is used. As Stephen Covey would say, this creates a win/win situation—both the seller and buyer win.

Above all, use extreme caution when using a credit card. Percentage rates can be as high as 50 percent if you end up paying compounded interest on a delinquent account. The road to financial health is paved with discarded credit cards.

Take a Pill if You're Ill

If you're sick, really sick, you go to the doctor, right? Sometimes the doc will put you in the hospital. Sometimes you may even require surgery. The same is true with our financial health. If we're a little sick, we read a book like this one and apply the principles. Doing this can help us recover. If financial hospitalization is required, we go to a nonprofit credit counseling agency to help us work out a recovery plan. To locate one of these agencies, call the Consumer Credit Counseling Service at 1-800-388-2227.

Don't wait to get help until you need major surgery. Attorneys fees and the blight of bankruptcy are expensive and embarrassing. The negative consequences of instant gratification are long-lasting.

Savings

Mary Hunt says in *The Financially Confident Woman,* "Saving money is its own reward. However, it has additional fringe benefits. Saving money is probably the best antidote for overspending" (Nashville: Broadman and Holman Publishers, 1996, p. 81). This comes from a woman who was $100,000 in debt—she knows about overspending.

In order to be "buff" (ask your teenager) financially, we should try to save from 5 to 10 percent of our net income. Keep in mind, we're talking savings here, not investing. A savings account allows us to purchase those unexpected items without debt. It also allows us the luxury of time in seeking the best buy.

The Miracle of Compounding Interest

Albert Einstein once called compounding interest the eighth wonder of the world. It doesn't take much to make money with compounding interest. Look at the chart showing what $1.00 a day will yield. You could give up your daily candy bar and soda—it will help more than your waistline!

As you can see by the chart, $1.00 a day invested for ten years at 10 percent interest will yield $6,145! Higher interest rates tend to be more speculative, so beware of the risks involved. You'll see it's worth the effort to save your dollar a day.

		\multicolumn{4}{c}{A DOLLAR A DAY}

YEARS	TOTAL INVESTED	\multicolumn{4}{c}{CUMULATIVE RETURN}
		5%	10%	15%	20%
10	$3,600	$4,658	$6,145	$8,257	$11,283
20	7,200	12,331	22,781	44,917	93,290
30	10,800	24,968	67,815	207,698	689,335
40	14,400	45,781	189,722	930,482	5,021,546
50	18,000	80,060	519,732	4,139,793	36,509,163

Figure 6

Start Saving Early

Look at our next illustration, which shows what investing $50 a month will do based on 10 percent interest compounded monthly. You'll see the person who starts saving early will yield bigger returns than the person who starts saving later (and pays more years). It's simple math, and it's simply astounding!

AGE		Saves Early			Saves Late		
21		$600	$600		0	0	
22		600	1,386		0	0	
23		600	2,185		0	0	
24		600	3,063		0	0	
25		600	4,029		0	0	
26		600	5,092		0	0	
27		600	6,262		0	0	
28		600	7,548		0	0	
29		0	8,303		600	600	
30		0	9,133		600	1,386	
31		0	10,046		600	2,185	
32		0	11,051		600	3,063	
33		0	12,156		600	4,029	
34		0	13,372		600	5,092	
35		0	14,709		600	6,252	
36		0	16,179		600	7,548	
37		0	17,798		600	8,962	
38		0	19,578		600	10,519	
39		0	21,535		600	12,231	
40		0	23,689		600	14,114	
41		0	26,057		600	16,185	
42		0	28,663		600	18,464	
43		0	31,529		600	20,970	
44		0	34,683		600	23,727	
45		0	38,151		600	26,760	
46		0	41,964		600	30,096	
47		0	46,160		600	33,765	
48		0	50,777		600	37,802	
49		0	55,854		600	42,242	
50		0	61,440		600	47,126	

Figure 7

Banking

All bank accounts are not created equal. When it comes to finding a bank, look for a free account. It may take a few phone calls, but there are banks that offer no monthly service charges when you maintain a minimum balance. Make sure this minimum balance is determined by your monthly average. Otherwise, you could have service fees charged against your account if your daily balance falls below the minimum for even one day during the month. Also look for banks that offer free checks. Expect a functional check rather than a fancy one. If you can't find free checks, then buy them from a check printer like Current (800-533-3973) or Checks in the Mail (800-733-4443). You can save as much as 60 percent over what the banks charge.

When selecting a bank, ask about the automated teller machine (ATM) services they offer. Many will not charge a fee for withdrawals on ATMs using the bank's system. Find out about the availability of these machines across your state and the country. You want to minimize the unnecessary transaction fee for using a different machine.

Watch the Teller

Just as a professional grocery shopper will closely watch the checker and review receipts at home, the professional bank client should do the same. Banks, tellers, and computers are not infallible. It's preferable to make all cash deposits in person. Better yet, use the direct deposit service your company offers. Keep all the receipts for deposits and withdrawals—including ATM receipts.

We were traveling one time and unexpectedly needed some cash. The ATM machine we used denied our request because of some glitch in the system. I kept the receipt. When our bank statement arrived, we found they had removed this money from our account. Thankfully, we still had our receipt to prove the error, and it was corrected. It was a $200 ATM mistake.

Bouncing

Bouncing checks can spell H-O-S-P-I-T-A-L for those inflicted with this financial flu bug. Most banks charge anywhere from $10 to $30 for a bounced check. Then, you are subject to the merchant's charge for handling your bad check—a minimum of $20. Bouncing two checks a month could cost you $1,300 a year!

Some tips to help avoid bouncing checks include the need for overdraft privileges. If you are prone to the bounce thing, then check around for banks that offer this service. Also, for you "right-brainers," who tend to do minimal calculations and record-keeping, duplicate checks are a must. Finally, when your account gets to the danger zone, make it a policy to limit your spending to cash only.

This doesn't include criminal charges and penalties that can be legally leveled against the perpetual bad-check writer. It's a crime to write bad checks. It costs your financial health.

Bonus Tip—Nonbanks

You may want to consider the nonbank option. Credit unions can be the better choice for many reasons. They offer cheaper interest rates and fees to their members because they serve the interest of their membership rather than accumulating massive profits. They tend to be smaller, thus providing personalized service.

By definition, credit unions are nonprofit organizations; they have a keen interest in serving their members. This means they tend to have more stringent lending requirements and maintain higher standards in the loan-to-deposit ratio. There's a national credit union organization I've investigated. They can help you find a credit union you may qualify to join. Write: Credit Union National Association, P.O. Box 431, Madison, WI 53701.

"9-1-1? I Need an EMT—ASAP!"

Tips to Saving on Energy, Medical, and Telephone Expenses

H ave you ever called 9-1-1? We have. Our house is an opportunity for an accident waiting to happen. We've been spared so many near-misses that I know our guardian angels work overtime. When I say we've called 9-1-1, I don't really mean Bob or I haved called. I mean other folks have called on our behalf—little folks.

About a year ago I opened my door, a sticky banana bread spoon in hand, to two military policemen. "Ma'am, did you dial 9-1-1?"

"No, uh, I didn't call you. There must be some mistake."

They were honor graduates of the Police Academy and, apparently, star pupils of Course 2401 in *Insistence and Persistence*. "Well, if you don't mind, we'd like to come in and take a look around."

I found out later that their course on *Hiding Criminals* (Course 3302) trained them to be suspicious of women holding sticky banana bread spoons. After all, there could be a criminal hiding behind the door, holding an egg beater to her head.

So they came into our home. They saw a mound of dirty laundry in the washroom and walked across the sticky kitchen floor. When they went to the back bedroom, they found Jonathan and Joshua, right in the middle of Mama's chocolate stash. The Mischief Brothers were holding a telephone. There was a chocolate fingerprint on the preprogrammed button marked "9-1-1."

Philip was particularly impressed with their shiny boots and the guns they wore. He gave them a plastic bag full of fresh slices of banana bread. I supposed they left to study up on *Criminal Behavior in the Young Child*, Course 4404.

The doorbell rang again the next day. I opened the door, an egg beater in my hand, to two military policemen. "Did you call 9-1-1, ma'am?"

I couldn't believe it. *They're back AGAIN?*

"No, and I took the preprogrammed button off our phone so the babies couldn't dial you again."

My mind raced, evaluating all the possibilities. *The babies are asleep, they couldn't have called.*

I needed more information. "Are you sure the call came from our home?" I asked, thoroughly confused.

"Yes, ma'am."

Daniel is at soccer practice, that leaves...

"Philip!" I called. He was in the schoolroom—by the phone.

Six-year-old Philip walked into the hallway, very slowly. "Did you call 9-1-1?" I demanded.

The little informant looked ashamed. "Yes." He stared at his shoes.

"Why, Philip? Why?" I asked incredulously.

He was visibly embarrassed. He spoke quietly, his voice barely audible. "I liked their boots—and guns. They're cool."

I gave the cops some freshly baked bread and they left.

Now, you may not have a great need for tips on how to dial 9-1-1. If you do feel the need for instruction, ask your local four-year-old. You may not need professional help from the police or an Emergency Medical Technician (EMT). But if you look a little closer at the following tips, I think you'll see that we all can use help in the area of EMT—Energy, Medical, and Telephone Expenses—in or out of emergencies.

Tips to Saving on Energy, Medical, and Telephone Expenses

Electricity and Energy Costs

There are almost as many ways to save on electricity as there are ways for the Kay children to create new fodder for their mom's books. I'll list a few, and I'm sure you can think of others.

- Check your windows and doors for air leaks. Use sealer tape to seal leaks.
- Clean system filters regularly and maintain heating and air conditioning units.
- Attic insulation should be at least six inches deep; it will save 10 percent.
- Keep thermostats set at moderate comfort—68° to 70° in winter and 74° to 78° in summer. This can save as much as 40 to 50 percent in hot climates and 12 percent in cooler climates.
- Lower the heating and cooling systems when your home is vacant for more than eight hours.
- Use a clock-operated thermostat.

More Energy Savers

- Have your local power company perform a free energy survey. Ask them about low-cost community programs to insulate your home.
- Stop the dishwasher after the wash cycle, or use the economy cycle. The warmth from the wash cycle will dry the dishes.
- Change the vacuum cleaner bag to improve efficiency. It saves electric energy—and human energy, too.
- Use your main oven for large food items. Bake as many dishes at once as possible.
- Use Crockpots and pressure cookers instead of the oven.
- Clean dust from refrigerator and freezer coils.
- Consider the Energy Guide labels on a new appliance before you purchase it.
- Consider installing storm windows and doors.

Still More Energy Savers

- Use blankets for warmth at night. Snuggle your Beloved.
- Turn off the TV. Play games with your babies.
- Close the damper on the fireplace when not in use.
- Wear a sweater.

- Wear cotton in the hot months.
- Keep the lint filter clean in your dryer.
- Use the "manual-operated dryer" outside. Buy extra clothespins.
- If you're not using it, turn it off!

Water

- Set hot water to a moderate setting of around 120°. This keeps the water hot enough to wash clothes but cool enough to keep from badly scalding little hands.
- Wrap the water heater with an insulation kit.
- Buy a water-restricted shower head to give plenty of water and little waste.
- Periodically drain the water heater from the bottom to remove sediments and allow for more efficient operation.

More Savings on Water

- Use your dishwasher, clothes washer, and dryer FULL to save water and electricity.
- Use cold water in your laundry. Current soaps on the market will clean your lightly soiled clothing easily without hot water.
- Try using less laundry detergent. Depending upon the water hardness in your area, you could use half the amount you're currently using. The same applies to your dishwasher.
- Use the partial-load water level adjustment on your clothes washer to customize the water to your current need.
- Fix leaky toilets and faucets—especially the hot water faucets. One leaky faucet wastes over 1,300 gallons a year!
- Take a shower instead of a bath. This can save as much as 50 percent of the total hot water in your home.
- If you're going to be away from your home for more than three days, turn off the hot water heater.
- Coordinate baths to conserve hot water. It takes 10 percent of the hot water in the tank to heat the lines to the bathroom. If you run the herd in and out of the shower and bath in the same hour, you'll save money.
- Read your utility bills each month and check the meters for accuracy.
- Water your lawn in the early morning hours and only once a week (if possible).
- Fill a quart-size plastic milk or juice bottle with water. Put it in your

toilet tank. This fills up space—you use less water to flush.

Medical Cost Savings

- Prevention is the best cure. Take care of yourself. Eat right and exercise. Take vitamins. Read up on herbs. Rest. Drink caffeine-free coffee and eat low-fat sugarless chocolate.
- Maintain your recommended body weight through common sense eating and exercise.
- Make friends with your doctor. Bring him or her oatmeal cookies and skim milk. Find someone you can trust before you need them.
- Choose a doctor who believes in preventive medicine.
- Find a doctor who will answer minor health questions over the phone.
- Follow your doctor's prescription. (For example, dietary restrictions or taking antibiotics.)
- Have a good health insurance plan.
- Don't use doctors excessively.
- When selecting a hospital, shop around—not all hospitals charge the same.
- Ask for an itemized hospital bill.
- Ask for routine tests to be done before hospital admission.
- Ask your doctor if day surgery is a possibility.

More Medical Savings

- Teach your children to brush their teeth and floss properly.
- Have regular dental checkups for every member of your family.
- Get a second opinion for surgery or extensive dental work.
- Question your doctor (your friend) about medical costs in advance.
- Educate yourself about medical issues to determine the value of the care you receive.
- Shop around for prescriptions, taking advantage of transfer specials and—coupons!
- Ask about prescription cash discounts.
- Ask for the generic version of your prescription.

Still More Medical Savings

- Eliminate smoking.
- Eliminate alcohol.
- Eliminate fatty foods and sugars.

- Drink plenty of water (eight eight-ounce glasses a day is ideal).
- Maintain a positive attitude.
- Get a physical at least once every three years.
- Get children's shots at the county health office.
- Ask your doctor for free samples of your needed medication.
- Laugh a lot.
- Laugh a whole lot.

Telephone Savings

- Write a letter.
- Use free email. We use Juno, available by writing New Members Dept., 120 W. 45th St., NY, NY 10036. Or call 1-800-654-JUNO.
- Check to see if there's a toll-free number for the long-distance call you'll make by dialing the toll-free operator at 1-800-555-1212.
- Dial direct; don't ask an operator for assistance whenever possible.
- Ask your operator for credit on wrong numbers and disconnects.
- Choose a long-distance carrier that bills in six-second increments.
- Avoid prepaid calling cards, which are usually more expensive.
- Don't call during the most expensive hours (Monday through Friday between 8:00 A.M. and 5:00 P.M.).
- Check your bill carefully; get credit for calls you didn't make.
- Evaluate your need for a cell phone.
- Use the cell phone for emergencies only.
- Use your phone book. Directory assistance is no longer a free call.

Here we are at the end of Section Two already! I hope you've found the information helpful and practical. Remember, you don't have to apply all these tips at once—just trying a couple of tips a week will send you on your way down the savings highway.

SECTION 3

Share

In one of our many moves, we were stationed in Alamogordo, New Mexico, for only three months. We lived in a *tiny* apartment called *The Alamo Apartments*. When the people downstairs smoked a cigarette—we inhaled the fumes. When our neighbor next door watched the news—we heard sports highlights. When the Kay herd ran up the stairs to our apartment—the entire building shook. Yes, it was small, it was old, and it was a tough assignment.

We chose to look at our "Alamo" time as a period of great opportunity for personal growth. When we think we're facing a tough challenge or we complain our house is too small, we've learned to say, "Remember the Alamo!" It helps put life in perspective.

The only redeeming factors in this scenario were the fellowship we found in a local church and the new friends we made. One of my new friends, Laurie, suffered a miscarriage during that time and was bedridden for several days. So I took her a meal. It was not that difficult; I just made a double portion of Chicken Spaghetti, some French bread, and a batch of Snickerdoodles. She was more than surprised—she was overwhelmed.

So was I, when she said, "What a delightful blessing. I've been in church for ten years, and this is the first time I've ever had anyone bring me a meal."

She was not a casual participant. Her family attended Sunday mornings, Sunday evenings, and Wednesday nights. It's known as being there "every time the doors are open."

Amazing. It's not as if they'd only been to one church all their lives. They, too, were a military family. They'd been stationed in several places and attended a local church at each assignment. Yet during the births of babies and bouts of illness, when they moved into a community and when they moved out, no one thought to bring them a meal. From what I've heard in my travels, they're not alone.

You may even want to ask yourself a few questions. Have you ever taken a meal to anyone? Does your office, play group, neighborhood, or church have an organized food tree? Have you ever been the means of a "delightful blessing" to someone in need?

I believe that even in the midst of our Alamo experiences, God has a plan. He wants us to get beyond ourselves, reach out to a neighbor, and help people in need.

Personally, I believe that if a small percentage of our community practiced these principles, there wouldn't be a need for the current extensive welfare programs. I'll issue you a personal challenge: Look around you, find those in need, and "Remember the Alamo!"

Our time at the Alamo provides the backdrop for the last part of the book. This final section focuses on the foundations of sharing. It mixes the philosophical with the practical. We'll take a peek at tips on how to find satisfaction in living a simple lifestyle, and you'll discover opportunities to apply solid financial principles. Hopefully, by the time you complete this book, you'll find yourself equipped—and eager—to share what you've learned with others.

In Texas, We Don't Throw Grits in a Wok

Tips to Sharing on a Budget

I got my first gray hairs when I was twelve years old—the same time other girls were getting their first bras. A few years ago, I gave into that old '70s commercial jingle where the model sang, *"I'm gonna wash that gray right out of my hair, I'm gonna wash that gray right out of my hair, and send it on its way."* My newly dyed mane made me feel twenty-something again. Energized, I set off to conquer the food store, while my Beloved watched the children.

Throughout the store, I was suddenly aware of men looking at me and smiling. I smoothed my hair with my hand. *It must be my youthful appearance.* Some of them looked quickly and then looked away. I shrugged my shoulders and decided, *It must be because I'm so embarrassingly beautiful.*

After two hours in the store, I drove home and burst in the door. I couldn't wait to tell Bob about my good bargains. He stopped me short. "Beloved," he said as he pointed in my direction, "the second button of your blue-jean dress is unbuttoned." I looked down at the alleged button—the critical button. I'd just shared Victoria's Secret with the entire supermarket.

It's great to feel pretty, oh, so pretty. It's also nice to feel the satisfaction that comes from saving money. But if we leave it there—we run the risk of accentuating what could be a *secondary* theme. Saving money is only a by-product of a greater principle—sharing with others. My friend Kyong helped me discover this truth.

Kyong is a military bride from Korea. When I met her, she was new to the United States and barely knew English. Since my Korean leaves a lot to be desired, we had difficulty understanding one another. But we had one thing in common: we both had a special relationship with God. She served Him in her small Korean congregation, and I did the same in my large contemporary church.

She knew nothing about *Shop, Save, and Share* seminars. Let's be frank, I had a hard time with "pass the egg rolls, please." How could I possibly tackle "a store coupon can usually be used in conjunction with a manufacturer's coupon?"

One day she came to my house visibly upset. "What's wrong, Kyong?" I asked.

She shook her head sadly. She struggled through the language as she answered, "Oh...Ellie. My...puh minustah."

"Your minister?" I asked, "What's wrong with him?"

She thought awhile, then haltingly explained. "I...go...his howse today. I...look...his cupboards, his frig-a-ra-tor. He...has no food."

I was confused. "No food? How come your minister has no food?"

Her face reddened. "The...deacons, they for-get. So...I take him some...my food."

Sometimes I'm gently tapped on the shoulder when I need to share. This occasion was obvious—it was not a gentle nudge. It was like a family-sized can of fruit cocktail hit me in the head. Kyong's plight got my attention.

Immediately, I went through my cupboards and began pulling out food. *I have four boxes of rice; great. I can give two of these. Three bags of flour. I'll donate one.* This continued until I had ten bags of groceries from my storehouse.

There is blessing in giving from our abundance. There's even greater blessing in giving out of our need. This time I gave out of my abundance. Sometimes I give Old Mother Hubbard style. You remember the nursery rhyme, don't you?

Old Mother Hubbard went to the cupboard
to give her poor dog a bone.
When she got there,
the cupboard was bare
so her poor dog had none.

Even when the cupboard is pretty bare, there's usually *something* to give those in need.

As I gathered these groceries, I came across a bottle of Nakano rice vinegar. I remembered that bottle. I got it free in the store two weeks earlier. I had a store coupon that read, "BUY NAKANO RICE VINEGAR, GET LETTUCE FREE." As you remember from chapter 4, a store coupon can *usually* be used in conjunction with a manufacturer's coupon. The vinegar was on sale for 99¢, and I had a manufacturer's coupon for 50¢ off, which was doubled by the store. The result? Both items were free.

I brought home a bottle of vinegar I thought I'd never use. Since I grew up in the country of Texas, my family didn't know how to cook oriental food, although I enjoy eating it. What can I say? In Texas, we don't throw grits in a wok.

I took the useless vinegar in order to get the needed lettuce. In the grocery store that day, when I put the Nakano rice vinegar in my cart, I didn't know it was going to be used to provide for someone in need, someone who probably used rice vinegar every day.

What a delightful experience to see God's hand in such a personal way. I learned the primary benefit of saving money that day: it is to experience the joy of having plenty to give away.

She extends her hand to the poor;
and she stretches out her hands to the needy
Proverbs 31:20

You may wonder how you can give when you're on a budget, and I can relate. As I've said before, on a $200-month grocery budget, I saved our family well over $8,000 last year. At the same time, I was able to give 100 bags of groceries (the equivalent of $1,000) to people in need. It can be done and done well!

Tips to Sharing on a Budget

Abundant Sharing

The beauty of the *Shop, Save, and Share* system is that there's plenty to go around. Once I went to the store when they were revamping the deodorant aisle. They had to get rid of dozens of perfectly good boxes of deodorant and had marked them down to $1.00 each. I had several 50¢-off coupons, and when they were doubled, it made the item free. I got sixteen brand-name deodorants for nothing but my coupon labor. Even if I had a basic hygiene problem, I couldn't use that much antiperspirant. There are many such items you'll get free, and they're easy to give away.

Look through your closets, garage, and storage shed. You may find an abundant supply of clothing, toys, and even furniture to donate to non-profit organizations. In turn, they'll distribute the items to those in need. The gift you give keeps giving.

Share Trial-Size Products

If a coupon specifically states: *Not Good on Trial Size* or *Good Only on 16-Count or Larger*, then the coupon must be used according to the listed terms. If there are no limitations, then use the coupon on a trial-size item to get it free or for a few pennies. I regularly pick up free trial-size toothpaste, lotion, deodorant, shampoo, conditioner, Band-Aids, Q-tips, hair spray, styling gel, shaving cream, laundry soap, tea, aspirin, medicines, razor blades, tampons, panty shields, cereals, drink mixes, popcorn—the list goes on and on. These are the best items to donate because the receiving organization can share them with many different people.

Share Buy One/Get One Free Products

If these specials are scanned at the register at half price, you can use a coupon for each item. For example, I once purchased Kellogg's Corn Flakes on a buy one/get one free special, and the store scanned the item at half price. The price was two for $1.99, or 99¢ each. I had a 50¢-off coupon for each item and was allowed to use two coupons. This double-coupon store doubled the value of each coupon, and I got both boxes free—one to keep and one to give away.

As we saw in chapter 4, if a store has this same sale and uses a store coupon or a clipless coupon (usually a frequent shopper card), a coupon for each item is usually allowed. The only time you cannot use two coupons for a buy one/get one free special is when the first item scans the cash register at full price and the second item scans at .00. So watch those sales to save and share.

Keep a Record of Your Sharing for Uncle Sam

While tax laws change each year, at press time the law allows income tax deductions for grocery and household goods contributions. The $1,000 worth of groceries we contributed to charitable organizations and the $800 in clothing, furniture, and miscellaneous items we donated last year were included on our income tax return. Sometimes you can get more from a charitable contribution than you can acquire from holding a garage sale. However, you must show proof of your donation, and you must itemize your deductions—showing donations that exceed the standard deduction.

The best method of recording these contributions is a twofold process: (1) keep your grocery receipt (or a photocopy of it) with the donated items highlighted, and make an itemized list of household goods and clothing contributions, and (2) ask the recipient for a tax-deductible receipt. The Salvation Army will give you an IRS-approved document listing high and low thrift-shop prices for various articles of clothing. To be safe in the event of an audit, I usually pick a value in the middle. This way, I can take the deductible allowed and I'm within the limits set by the IRS.

We have letters stating the total annual value of donated groceries and household goods from each of the organizations we contributed to. For needy families in our church and community, we donated these anonymously (the families didn't know who gave them these necessities) through the church. That way, the church kept a record of our donations and they distributed the goods. The same applies to most of the organizations listed in the next section. I suggest that you check with a Certified Tax Consultant each season to verify current tax laws.

Watch the Cash Register for Free Items

Some stores have a scan guarantee—either the item scans the accurate price or you get it free. This makes a fun game for a half-wit. I watch those prices like a hawk and ring a cowbell when they scan wrong. Of course, it's kind of embarrassing if *I'm* wrong, but it's a great savings when I'm right. Once, I got a $15.97 double bag of diapers FREE when it scanned at $15.99. Yee haw! I've received *many* other free products, as well, by watching the scan.

Share a Rebate

Chapter 9 goes into great detail about refunding, its limitations, and refund fraud. When I say *share a rebate*, I mean donate that rebate to a family in need. For example, when you get a coupon for a free bottle of picante sauce—donate that product to a local food shelf. I got free toy trucks through Kellogg's one year. I donated those trucks to the Toys for Tots program. You can't get a tax-deductible receipt for that one item, since it was free—but you can make some little children (and their parents) very happy.

Just another reminder—don't trade, sell, or even give away completed rebates. The manufacturer *usually* limits the refund to *one per household* and any other use could constitute fraud. It's just not worth the risk, and more importantly, it's wrong. Donate those items you're getting free and don't be greedy.

Make Two and Share One

Often I'll make two casseroles—one to eat and one for the freezer. Spaghetti pie is one of our favorite leftover meals and the recipe can easily make two meals. The same goes for my pumpkin and banana breads, Snickerdoodle cookies, and anything else I can freeze. "Meal in a Loaf" is a favorite simple and inexpensive sharing meal. I make Easy French Bread and roll (jelly-roll style) meats and cheeses into the loaf. This original recipe is great for picnics and wonderful to have in my freezer for a new friend moving into the neighborhood.

Developing an attitude of sharing is the basic idea behind these tips. Soon you'll come up with your own ideas, and I hope you'll send them to me—I'm always *in the market* for new ideas!

True Giving Means Having a Half-Wit's Memory

You know you've developed an attitude of sharing when you don't keep track (other than for Uncle Sam) of your giving. I've honestly forgotten many of the people to whom I've given clothing, cakes, and cross-stitch. My friend Loretta is much the same way. She forgets who she's given what. Of course, she also forgets where she put the car keys—and the kids. She gives away meals, opens her home to people who need a place to live, and feeds traveling herds. This dear friend does all of these things without an organized bone in her body. Her husband of twenty-six years, Daryl, is very patient. Loretta says with conviction, "If God did give some organization to me, I've probably misplaced it somewhere and can't remember where I put it."

Give Out of Your Need

As we saw earlier, there's a time to give out of our abundance and a time to give Old Mother Hubbard style. I've found tremendous satisfaction in giving out of our need. Even when I don't have much to share, I've learned to give a little.

Sometimes the timing to provide a meal is impossible. Other times it's inconvenient. Look deep within yourself and decide whether taking a meal to the lady up the street is *impossible* or *inconvenient.* If it takes a little stretch on your part to donate your time to meet this need, then just do it! The satisfaction found in helping others, even when it's hard, is worth the inconvenience.

Shared Knowledge Is Wealth Multiplied

Some people are in financial distress due to a lack of understanding. They don't know *how* to save money and they feel there's no hope for them. Remember the old saying, "You can give a man a fish and feed him for a day, or you can show him how to fish and feed him for a lifetime"? Why don't you consider giving some fishing lessons? Share the insights you've received from your experience. Give that friend a copy of this book. Show your neighbor your latest grocery receipt or garage sale bargain—a picture is worth a thousand words!

Every Mom Is a Working Mom

Tips for Working Moms

I try to be a pretty easygoing person—but I wasn't always that way. Part of the reason I've mellowed is because I've learned two major lessons: (1) life is too short for high-maintenance relationships, and (2) life is too short to let "ugly acting" people get to you.

So most of the time I won't rip your face off for asking an innocent question. Nevertheless, despite my resolve to be laid back and not be a high-maintenance person, there's still one question I'm asked that tends to get under my skin. THE question is usually asked by someone who's trying to get to know me or as part of polite discourse—they certainly don't mean to "act ugly." They probably don't mean to offend—but try as I might, the question still bothers me. The question is (drum roll, please): *Do you work?*

Do I work? Do you call getting up at 5:30 A.M. each day and dropping exhausted into bed at 11:30 P.M. work? What about doing fourteen loads of laundry a week, keeping a neat home, and schooling five children? Do you suppose that could be called "work"? How about feeding, dressing, and bathing said children, exercising four times a week, baking, and cooking daily? Is that just "sitting around"? Add to these regular activities all my military obligations and functions, shopping sales, organizing seminars, and writing a book—you bet your sweet little Justin Red Roper Boots I work!

No, that's *not* what they meant when they asked the question. These people really want to know if I work *outside the home*. There are days when I try to convince Bob to let me put on his flight suit and helmet and go to his "work." How can you possibly call operating a fighter—with the adrenaline pumping and the excitement of flying low and fast—work? Would you call riding a roller coaster for a living anything but *fun*?

Whether you work inside or outside the home—every mom is a working mom. The following tips will help your family assess the financial status of a mom working outside the home. Hopefully, the following ideas will help you synergize your time and energy and make for more productive time with your little mice. All of us have one thing in common—we *all* work. Some moms work in the Rat Race and others chase mice for a living.

Tips for Working Moms

Compensation

Our work around the house, including care of the children, earns a different kind of compensation than work outside the home. Compensation can't be measured in dollars and cents exclusively. One woman may stay home because of the satisfaction of influencing her children. She doesn't want a child-care provider to see those first steps and hear that first word. She has a choice, and her decision is to stay home.

Other women work outside the home for the same reason. They'd rather share the joys of motherhood and continue to find satisfaction in working in a job outside the home. She, too, has a choice.

Then there's the last group of women, who want to stay at home but feel they do not have a financial choice in the matter. While I'm not going to enter the "to work/or not to work" debate, I do want to provide some facts and tips that will help this last group of women see what their choices really are. This can help them make their decision from a financial perspective. It's up to each family to decide where mom will center her work activities—inside or outside the home.

Sally the Stenographer

How would you like to do all your work around the house, all the volunteer activities in church and school, and work outside the home as well? Maybe some of you already have this lifestyle. Now, how would you like to do all of this with *no financial compensation whatsoever*? I'm not talking about volunteer work. We don't expect a financial return for that kind of work—that's why it's called volunteering. I'm talking about the other work you do—outside of the home. It's ridiculous—why would anyone work hard outside the home for no compensation? Well, that's exactly what Sally was doing—and she didn't even know it.

Sally the stenographer needed to work outside the home. Her family couldn't make ends meet without her financial contribution. Sally made an average wage of $6.50 per hour and felt she contributed to the family's finances. She only had one child in daycare, traveled a short distance to work, and paid no state income taxes. Then Sally attended one of my seminars and was challenged with the idea of "crunching the numbers." She completed the form on the next page and was shocked. (Figure 8)

The amazing fact Sally discovered was that by working full time—*she was in the red by $7 per month!* She didn't realize how those extra pizza nights (because she was too tired to cook), the trips to the beauty salon (to maintain a professional hairstyle), and all those lunches (away from home) added up! Sally realized she needed to make some dramatic adjustments. So she began taking her lunch to work and cut back on trips to the beauty shop. She found this didn't benefit her much. The sacrifices allowed her to make $30 a week. Wasn't her exertion and sacrifice (and 50 hours a week away from home) worth more than a mere $30? She decided there was a better use of her energy and quit her job outside the home.

But Sally didn't stop there. She implemented some of the ideas from this book and is financially ahead of her fellow stenographers. She has less stress in her life and the freedom to contribute to her family's financial needs through saving money in the home. (After all, a penny saved is more than a penny earned.) Sally discovered the incredible joy of sharing with those in need. She contributes her time and groceries to an eternal investment—people's lives. You see, not all compensation is measured in dollars and cents.

Crunch the Numbers

You'll notice Sally is a bare-minimum example. When you crunch your own numbers, you may discover other factors, like your family is in a higher tax bracket because your job puts you over the edge. You may commute farther than Sally, have more than one child in childcare, and eat more convenience foods. You may feel the pressure to have manicured nails, expensive suits, or any number of additional personal perks (because you work so hard and deserve those extras). The important thing (because you work so hard and deserve those extras). The important thing is to accurately assess your net usable income.

Once you come up with a figure, ask the big question. Is my time, energy, and effort worth _____ dollars a week? You'll be surprised at how painless it is to cut back and save your family a significant amount of money. It's not magic; it requires work and dedication. You work hard now; you just have to decide if it's worth it. After all, not all compensation is measured in dollars and cents.

Working Mother Chart Exercise

Figure 8

Sally the Stenographer

Gross Income per week	Sally's	Yours
(40 hrs @ $6.50/hr) Less:	$260.00	_____
Tithe (10%)	$26.00	_____
Federal Income Tax (15%)	$35.00	_____
Social Security Tax (6.65%)	$20.00	_____
Transportation (10 trips of 8 mi @ 30¢/mi)	$24.00	_____
Childcare (1 child)	$75.00	_____
Meals/coffee (@ $6.00/day)	$30.00	_____
Convenience foods at home	$25.00	_____
Extra clothing (includes cleaning and cosmetics)	$9.00	_____
Beauty shop	$14.00	_____
Other ("I owe it to myself") items	$5.00	_____
Total Expenses	$267.00	_____
Net Usable	$7.00	_____

Time Spent:		
On the job	40 hours	_____
Lunch	5 hours	_____
Travel	5 hours	_____
Hours away from home	50 hours	_____

Stress Busters

Whether you work inside or outside of the home, all moms have a certain amount of stress that goes along with the territory. The following list can give you a boost. As a matter of fact, psychologists—who routinely advise their clients to practice these tips in order to reduce stress—comprised a surprising list of stress busters. Here are a few of my favorites.

• Throw away some junk.
• Give away some junk (see chapter 24).
• Sell some junk (see chapter 13).
• Simplify your life (see the next chapter).
• Say "no" to busywork (see chapter 23).
• Hug your children (see chapter 5).
• Laugh (see any chapter).
• Laugh a lot (see chapter 14).

Caroline Ingalls' Stress Buster

If all these fail to minimize stress in your life, then do what I call the "pioneer thing." Yep, the pioneer thing. When our foremothers settled the country out west, they lived off the land. They had a difficult existence and a shorter life expectancy than we have today. In other words—life was downright hard! After Ma Ingalls and her contemporaries spent the morning harvesting hog lard and making soap, they hauled water from the creek and boiled the baby's diapers. Every now and then, when junior smeared lard all over Ma's freshly swept dirt floor, and Laura dropped the clean diapers in the pig pen, even Caroline Ingalls (saint though she was) got a bit stressed.

Do you think she "worked"? You bet she did. She worked so hard that she had to do something to relieve the pressure. Otherwise, she'd end up at the funny farm—which was 2,000 miles due east.

There's nothing in the *Little House on the Prairie* books to substantiate my "pioneer thing" theory. Nonetheless, I believe I know how Ma coped with her difficult life. I firmly believe that when she was stressed, she put down her butter churn, told Mary to watch the children, and took a walk. She walked two miles or so, straight into the middle of the prairie. There wasn't another family living within ten miles in any direction. She raised her hands and looked up to the heavens. Then she yelled her guts out.

Afterward, Ma said a little prayer, straightened the loose strands of hair in her bun, and walked back home—ready to face another day of work.

Likewise, if you've got a cow pasture nearby, a prairie, or even a good patch of woods, just take yerself a lil' old walk and do the pioneer thing. It works for me—except when the neighbors call 9-1-1.

Benefits of Home Work

A lot of value has been taken away from women who work in the home since Caroline Ingalls' day. Back then, there were fewer choices, and women who worked in the home were supported by society and esteemed for their contributions to the home. I'm the first to say I don't want to go back to the "good old days." I understand hog lard is fairly difficult to store and the price of butter churns is outrageous.

On the other hand, a woman who chooses to stay at home, for all the right reasons, needs some affirmation now and then. These tips are for you. Here are a few of the benefits of home work.

• The mom who works at home can make more meals from scratch and save big bucks on food.
• Her children can have great snacks at school, because Mom has time to make them. The other children may gladly trade their fruit roll-ups for a homemade chocolate chip cookie.
• The family's consumer debt can be reduced due to a simpler lifestyle, active savings measures, and a relief from the pressures at work (outside the home) to have more, buy more, and pay more.
• Mom will have more time for her children and family activities.
• Her children learn the value of a dollar because Mom isn't too tired to take them to garage sales on Saturday morning.
• There's flexibility to take vacation time when the children are on break from school.
• Mom has the freedom to pursue new hobbies.

Tips for Moms Who Work Outside the Home

You've probably noticed that many of the tips in this chapter relate to a mom, period. No matter where she works. Well, I've worked outside the home at times, and I understand there is a time and place for gainful employment. Here are some tips that work for me when I'm working outside the home.

Child-care provider. Organize, on the computer, a basic child-care provider list. Update and add to these lists as you need them. This saves time and energy—it also reduces stress. If you don't feel comfortable with your children's care, then shop around. You have to feel good about their provider.

Assign chores to children within their abilities. We use a chore chart, and adjust the children's allowances according to the choices they make regarding their chores. Work teaches responsibility, and children need to learn this principle at an early age. Why, even Conan (baby Joshua) picks up his toy cars. Of course, he also throws them out the window—but he's still in training.

Plan easy meals ahead of time. This will save time, money, and stress. You might even want to try Once-A-Month Cooking (see book list). This is a great system that prepares the base of the month's meals in one long day of cooking. Beth Lagerborg and Mimi Wilson show us how to combine several meal portions in one preparation time and freeze them for later.

Exercise. My friends sometimes ask, "How on earth do you find the energy to do it all—and exercise?" My answer is simple. "If I don't exercise, I don't have the energy to do it all!" (Besides the basic fact that I don't really do it all.) You have to take care of yourself and your body. Maybe you can combine a brisk walk with your lunch hour or bike ride with the children after work. Weekends are a wonderful time to catch up on physical activity. Exercise is a great stress buster, too.

Pray. There is Someone who knows you by name. He sees your schedule and He cares about your day. He wants to help; all you have to do is ask Him. Since prayer is a two-way conversation, you'll need to take time to listen to what He has to say to you. Spending time in God's Word helps us understand His direction. I use Oswald Chambers' devotional classic *My Utmost for His Highest* and the Radio Bible Class devotional *Our Daily Bread* in my quiet times. They provide a Scripture, a story, and a thought for the day. *Our Daily Bread* is available through RBC Ministries, Grand Rapids, Michigan 49555-0001. Or you can visit them on the Internet at http://www.rbc.net.

Have a Plan

The most successful people in life have a plan regarding their work and their lives. People tell me they're amazed at how much work I get done each day. Every one of my days begins with time for planning and prioritizing. Minimizing the amount of time spent in front of the television greatly increases productivity. Organizing like chores in the same time-block helps kill as many birds with one stone as possible.

Even though I'm a list person, I try not to let my list control me. I pray over those "things to do" each day with this prayer. *Lord, please help me to get those things done today that are truly important. Help me to be content to let fall by the wayside those things that don't really matter.*

The Work That Matters Most

No matter where your work is centered, there is one investment that yields eternal dividends. That investment is in people. I believe that when I'm eighty years old, sitting in a quiet room for countless hours each day and clipping coupons, I'll look back on my life. Honestly, I don't believe I'll worry much about my work or accomplishments. The benefit of time will help me realize the work that mattered most—the investment I've made into the lives of others. Hopefully, there will be no regrets.

When you're old, you won't worry about earning more money. You won't wish you had closed more lucrative business deals or obtained that extra degree. I really don't believe you'll stew over failed cooking experiments, wish you drove a nicer car, or gone on that dream vacation. You won't agonize over Neiman's labels versus Kmart specials. The fact that you didn't exercise five times a week won't bother you much. Your main source of pain won't be the fact that you could never fit back into a size eight dress after having babies.

I think, if we have any regrets, they'll relate to the amount of time invested in *relationships*. We may long for the season when a parent was still around to talk and laugh with. We may wish we had taken the time to cuddle that munchkin, giving him his third drink of water and reading a second bedtime story. Your heart may twinge at the desire to have spent more time conversing with your spouse when you had the opportunity. The seasons of life pass so quickly, and we miss out if we don't take the time to invest in those around us.

After all is said and done, you'll wish you had made time for the people that matter most to you.

Simply Speaking— Let's Get a Grip!

Tips to Simplify Your Life

McDonald's is a hallowed spot for this little old gal from Texas. When my mom and I went shopping at Kmart, we usually took Abuela, my Spanish grandmother. This generous, hard-working woman often treated us to lunch at McDonald's from the money she earned laboring in the kitchen clean-up area of a retirement home. I remember standing in line, waiting for my 23¢ hamburger and singing the Big Mac song. *Two whole beef patties, special sauce, lettuce, cheese, pickles, onions, on a sesame seed bun.* If I was really good, Abuela would buy me a 15¢ Coke. If it were Christmas or my birthday, then I might get half of a hot apple pie for 21¢. Those were the days—simple pleasures in a simpler life.

Today our children are involved in more extracurricular activities than any previous generation. The "simple life" is just an old song at the opening of the movie remake *Father of the Bride.* Some of our lives are so complicated that figuring out an income tax return makes for a relaxing evening at home.

We have tons of options and opportunities that are often obstacles to the simple life. At the end of some days, I'm exhausted. And yet I feel as if I've only run the first leg of a 1,000-mile, 100-day race across the country. I know that every day this week will be just as demanding, just as action-packed, just as complex. Admittedly, there are times I long for the simple, Abuela-generated days of McDonald's and apple pies.

I'm not alone. At one time or another, everyone feels, as the air force says, "overtasked and undermanned."

Well, there's good news for complex lives: there's hope for us. If the research put into this chapter helps you as much as it helped me, then you won't feel as if you're still a few fries short of a complete happy meal. Let's learn together, how we can—simply speaking—get a grip!

Top Ten Tips to Simplifying Your Life

Tips From a Bunny

Ever since she was old enough to hold a crayon and find an empty wall, Bethany's been a writer. She's created some 5,247 works of art in her seven years on this planet. They're posted on our refrigerator, Bob's desk at work, my computer monitor, and the toilet seat cover. We've got our Bunny's "cottage industry products" on the rearview mirror in the car, the bathroom mirror, and my compact powder mirror. They are a reflection of her soul.

Sometimes she writes her feelings through pictures. As her language skills progress, she writes her thoughts as poems. Here's a poem she wrote when she was six to a pair of sisters in our neighborhood.

Friends
A Poem

No one is good as you two.
No one hass a Better Time,
You two.
And you two our the best ever.

Bethany Kay ©1997

Yes, I suppose I'm biased, but I think this little girl has talent. She writes, colors, and pastes her way into the hearts of friends and family, neighbors, and even acquaintances. Bethany has the uncanny ability to see the best in others. She encourages people when the world beats them down and leaves them for lost.

Assess the "A" List

We can learn something from a happy bunny. Take our schedules, for instance. If we think about the beautiful in the midst of an ugly, busy schedule, we, too, can bring simplicity out of complexity. Why not write a list of *everything* on your schedule for the past two weeks? List the regular commitments and responsibilities, the daily tasks, and the additional duties. Don't forget the activities of your child and your spouse; they impact your life, too. As a final note, add up the hours spent in front of the television and on the computer.

You should have a substantial list compiled at the end of this homework assignment. I sure did—I didn't realize I was doing so much *stuff* until it was written down. When we look at our lives in black and white, we have to ask the age-old question: "Why?"

Why am I spending so much time pursuing activities that are unimportant and not urgent? Aren't these time *wasters* in the scheme of life? Why do busywork, phone calls, and trivia take the place of planning, recreation, and relationship-building?

In *Seven Habits of Highly Effective People*, Covey says, "To say yes to important...priorities, you have to learn to say no to other activities, sometimes apparently urgent things." When we write these activities down on paper, we can prioritize and evaluate the importance of the "stuff" that fills our schedules—and our lives.

I'll go one step further and ask you about your "A list" or activities list. What activities are unimportant and yet still on your list? Do you have time for the important or only the urgent? Why not pray about your schedule? Why don't you ask your Father to help order your life? Why not ask Him to take the complex and make it a little simpler?

I'll end this "tip" with another Bunny poem. It was written when I was having a horrible, terrible, no good, very bad day. There wasn't a whole lot to like about me on that day. There wasn't an empty pasture to yell in—so my children were yelled at instead. Even though I asked for forgiveness, my outburst left me feeling like a failure. Later in the day, Bunny gave me this:

My Mama
A Poem

I love her so.
I love her like she was mom.
She still is.
She has a way to helpe me spell good.
The way I like it to be.
I love her so so so so so so so so so so much.
By your Bethany

Bethany Kay ©1997

Baubles, Bangles, and Beads

As a young teenager, I used to spend hours playing the "Catalog Game." I'd take a catalog and turn to the jewelry section. At each page, with the product prices covered, I'd ask myself a question, "If you could have any piece of jewelry on this page, which would you pick?" I'd hem and haw and then I'd pick my favorite. I'd check the price; if it was the most expensive piece on the page—I won! It proved I had good taste.

One day my dad caught me pouring over the catalog and laughed. "Oh, Ellie, you're one for baubles, bangles, and beads." The triple-B accessories can take over your life if you let them.

Guys don't have this problem. They put on a uniform, a suit and tie, or a T-shirt and jeans and they're set to go. Women, on the other hand, have to scrounge through their *bangles* to find their *baubles,* and then locate matching *beads.* Consider simplifying your life by having only two sets of jewelry: one set for every day and one for special occasions. Give away the rest and watch your jewelry frustration melt away.

Get Rid of the Junk

There's a basic philosophy at the Kay house about the stuff we accumulate over the years: *Junk has the ability to accumulate according to the amount of storage space available.* Several years ago, we moved to a house with extra storage. We thought, "Oh great—more space." At first we had some extra breathing room. In a matter of a few months, we filled the space with junk. We found ourselves once again overpowered by the

184

self-imposed pressure of STUFF!

Now I go through all the boxes *before* they make it into a storage room. We chuck the junk and have less stress. Every six months we sort through all five of the children's clothing, toys, and stuff—getting rid of the ties that bind and gag. Sure, it takes a full day's effort to purge ourselves of the perplexing pile. But the result is worth it—a refreshed soul.

It's the Little Things That Count

When we moved from New Mexico to upstate New York, we wanted to be inconspicuous travelers. However, we had to take enough clothing for four months (for seven people), food for the 3,000-mile trip, and equipment for the camper we were pulling. If you can picture it, we had a cherry red Suburban (with a massive travel pod on top) pulling a twenty-one-foot travel trailer (including five bicycles strapped on an exterior bike rack). There were kids hanging out the windows and Barney underwear flying in the wind (who stuck that in the trailer door?). We were inconspicuous, all right.

When people passed us on the highway, they were either laughing or shaking their heads. I felt a lot like "Granny" on *The Beverly Hillbillies*. All we needed was my rocker strapped on top of the luggage rack—but that's where Bob drew the line.

When we added up all the "little things" we needed for our trip and temporary living, we found we were hauling five thousand pounds—the bare minimum. Bob is a master packer. His motto: Stuff and cram.

It's amazing how all the little things in our life add up, clogging up the sleek machinery and draining us of our energy. Simplifying, even in little things, can help loads. I'll close out this chapter with a list of "little things." If you start thinking about your idea of simplicity, you'll come up with a lot more little things. In the process, I think you'll also find a lot more breathing room.

Drink Water

This little tip helps our waistlines, wallets, and well-being. We all know we should drink more water, but it has to become a habit—it doesn't come naturally. I've heard that if we do anything consistently for twenty-one days, it becomes a habit. At first, you have to remind yourself to practice the positive action. Day four or five seems to be the hardest. However, once this act is repeated regularly for a least twenty-one days— it becomes automatic.

Drinking water, as a habit, refreshes our physical bodies and makes us healthier. Drinking water saves all kinds of money spent at the grocery store on other beverages. Drinking water saves the hassle of recycling cans, plastics, and bottles. Drinking water is a little, refreshing way to simplify.

Turn Out the Intruder

Were you completely honest when you made a written list of your weekly activities? You did make a list, didn't you? If you are normal, you had anywhere from thirty to forty hours of television (or videos, computer games, or "surfing the net" time) on your schedule. Try keeping a media log, and keep track of each family member's time on the PC, video, or TV—for just a few days. You'll be amazed.

One of the reasons Bob and I get so much done each day is that we've turned out the intruder. For the first five years of our marriage, we refused to buy a television set. My father and brother brought their own TV to our house on Thanksgiving so they could have their football fix. We got a video monitor in year six and have a television now—but no cable.

It's so easy to let this intruder eat up family, relationship, and productivity time. I'll watch an occasional video while clipping coupons, or we'll watch a family video on special evenings. We don't have to rush around, catching up on responsibilities because we've wasted countless hours in front of the silly tube. Let's face it, a lot of the stuff on television is the same kind of stuff that fills our storage space—junk. Throw it out and get a life—the simple life.

Easy Care

Instead of buying clothing that has to be dry-cleaned, pressed, and starched—try buying easy-care clothing instead. Sometimes you don't have a choice, but often you can just as easily choose a wash-and-wear article of clothing as you can a dry-clean-only item. The time you spend running to the dry cleaner and the money you save on your $10 to $15 a week laundry bill is well worth the choice.

Quit Your Job

Have you ever had a job you despise? Have you ever prayed for a plague to overtake you (or your employer) so you didn't have to go in to work? Have you ever quit your job because you loathed your boss? Then at your next job you find your new supervisor is your former boss's evil twin brother, Skippy? Been there. Done that.

Shouldn't we be involved in jobs that utilize our God-given skills, talents, and gifts? Chuck Swindoll, in his radio program *Insight for Living*, said that when people operate within their (spiritual) gift, it is done "with ease and effectiveness." Think about it. Is your present job done with ease and effectiveness?

For a number of years my seminar engagements operated in a feast or famine cycle—my self-esteem followed the same pattern. When there were many speaking gigs I felt valued; when there were few—I felt as if I was "nothing more than" a wife and mother. Then God completely shut the door on speaking. For two years the load dropped from five presentations a *month* to only one a year. During that season, I learned that being a wife and mother was *everything* and the seminar stuff was *secondary*. Also, I learned to do my *primary* job, that of mothering, with ease and effectiveness. Then, and only then, did God restore speaking opportunities. As a matter of fact, the seminars had a greater purpose, power, and response than ever before. That famine season revealed a simple truth: God is the giver of all good gifts.

If you're not operating within your area of ease and effectiveness, look around. You may be operating outside your skill level. You may not be suited to your present job. You may have reached the place where you're no longer challenged. Or, as in my case, you may simply need to learn the lesson God wants to teach you in your present job.

Don't Say the "B" Word or I'll Scream

Tips to Creating a Workable Household Budget

The way my life usually works is that when I'm filled with pride—in comes a heavy dose of humility. I have need of patience, and there are opportunities through which patience can come. God is committed to my spiritual growth, and when I become so full of myself, He wants to see me emptied. So He gives me five children who are strong-willed and active. They present me with countless well-timed mishaps that require patience and perseverance. Sometimes I make the right choice and other times...well, I don't.

Maybe crazed toddlers aren't your problem. You might want to scream when someone mentions coupons. You may be one who runs for a sock to stuff in your mouth when you hear the cry, "The game's starting now," as you watch the 532nd sporting event of the season. Or you may react with impatience when we mention the "B" word—the family budget.

We're going to look at the highlights of a family budget. This list is not all-inclusive; it only provides a working outline of a typical household budget plan. If this chapter is not detailed enough for you, then you'll probably want to get a book like *The Family Budget Workbook* by Larry Burkett (Chicago: Moody Press, 1996).

Tips to Creating a Workable Household Budget

Assess Current Spending/Saving

On the next page, we've provided a budget form (Figure 9). You may make photocopies and fill in the blanks for your *current* spending levels. Be sure to include all debt accumulation, including credit cards, and read "More Hidden Bills" on page 191. As a matter of fact, it's a good idea to read the rest of this chapter before you complete this chart to unearth all those hidden debts.

Since the goal is to live *below* our means, we'll need to also allocate money for specific savings areas, and you'll see those on the chart, as well. If you're already saving, then you're ahead in the budget game.

Assess Net Income

This is the household income *after* state and federal income taxes and social security. Income includes salary, rents, notes, interest, dividends, any income tax refund, and other forms of income. Enter the total on the line "net income" on the budget form.

Where Are You?

Now take your net income and subtract your current spending to establish your overall family spending. Are you spending more (through credit) than you make each month? Are you spending everything you make (with nothing going into savings)? Are there unexplained gaps in your current spending levels? Did you know you were hitting the ATM that many times each month? Are you saving as much as you'd like to?

We have to start at the beginning, and the first three tips help us know where we are so we can have a better idea of where we're going.

Projected Budget

Look on the budget chart and fill in the column "projected budget" according to the percentage given. These figures are based on an average American's household income of around $20,000 to $38,000 a year. The percentages are guidelines and will vary according to family size, geographic location, and income.

This column gives a good idea of where to go with your budget. Take the difference between columns one and two to determine if your current spending levels are over or under the projected budget. This exercise will

BUDGET PAYMENT PER MONTH

ACCOUNT NAME	CURRENT SPENDING		PROJECTED BUDGET		DIFFERENCE		ACTUAL BUDGET	
Tithes/contributions (10%)								
Savings (10%)								
Clothing/Dry Cleaning (5%)								
Education/Misc. (5%)								
Food (10%)								
Housing/Utilities/Taxes (30%)								
Insurance (5%)								
Medical/Dental (4%)								
Recreation/Vacation								
Gifts/Christmas (6%)								
Transportation (15%)								
Net Income								

Figure 9

show you where you need improvement—if you're consistently going over budget. Some families think they're doing pretty well each month—saving as much as 10 percent—but then this exercise reveals the pattern of a gradually increasing debt load.

Compare your current spending column with the projected budget column to determine areas that need the most attention in your family's budget. Write the difference (either in the black or in the red) in column three.

Actual Budget

Using the projected budget as a guideline, establish an actual budget for your family. Your budget will be based on your family's size, geographical location, and income. In one family, Mr. Smith drove a company car, so his automobile expenses were slightly lower than average. They took this overage and carried it over to the servicing of their consumer debt. They took measures to cut their food budget (couponing, maybe?) and shopped around on insurance—thereby arriving at a workable budget for their family.

Hidden Bills

These are expenses that should be figured into the monthly budget in order to give your family an accurate assessment of where you're at in annual expenses. These include bills that may not come due on a monthly basis. Nevertheless, the budget should provide for the payment of these items. These debts also include insurance premiums, property and other taxes, retail credit, money owed to family and friends, doctor and dentist bills, magazine subscriptions, etc. There are blank spaces on the budget worksheet to fill in these expenses.

Still More Hidden Bills

Each category in our worksheet has hidden expenses you may not have considered. This is a complete, itemized list of costs that should be included in each of these categories.

Clothing/Dry Cleaning. New clothing and shoes, thrift-store bargains, garage-sale finds, dry cleaning, alterations, repairs, patterns, and sewing supplies.

Education/Miscellaneous. Tuition, books, music or other lessons, school supplies, newspaper, miscellaneous expenses (field trips, teachers' gifts, fund-raisers, etc.). The miscellaneous portion includes all other unbudgeted items and any debt payments.

Food. Groceries, and meals eaten outside the home.

Tithe/Charitable Donations. Church, civic, community donations.

Housing. Includes mortgage or rent, property taxes, utilities (including phone, gas, water, and electricity), cleaning supplies, labor costs/maid, lawn care, pool care, tools and repair, stationery, postage, household repairs, furniture and bedding, appliances, and garden equipment.

Insurance. The percentage provided assumes some employee insurance benefits. It also includes life, house, and health insurance.

Medical/Dental. Doctor, dentist, eyeglasses, medicines, and vitamins.

Recreation/Vacation and Gifts/Christmas. Baby-sitting, cameras and film, entertainment, movies, hobbies, pets, television, sporting goods, toys, all gifts, Christmas decorations and gifts, and vacations.

Savings. Savings accounts, savings for hidden debts and unexpected emergencies.

Transportation. Airline fares, bus and taxi fares, car payments and insurance, car repairs and licenses, gasoline, and oil.

Budget Busters

There are a few problem areas that can throw a budget off course in a matter of seconds—sending it reeling toward disaster. The use of debt, or credit, is the number one budget buster. I suggest you look at making your family's policy one of "cash only." Some families set up an envelope system for cash. Every two weeks, they place the budgeted amount of cash in envelopes marked "food," "entertainment," "gas," etc. When the money runs out—you're done until the end of the two-week period. A regular peek at the amount of cash left in each envelope is a vivid reminder of your budget commitments.

If you don't have the cash for that gorgeous new outfit on sale at your favorite store, then don't buy it. If you really can't afford to go out to eat four times a month, then only go twice. If it's not in your budget to fly the family out to your mother's for vacation, then drive or let Mom come to you. "Cash only" could be the single most important principle in sticking to an effective budget.

More Budget Busters

Impulse buying, as we've discussed earlier, is a temptation faced by almost everyone. Whether it's a candy bar or a Corvette—we've all given in to the craving at one time or another. There are ways to short-circuit this tendency within our natures, and one of the best ways is the thirty-day plan we discussed earlier. If it's not in your budget, then wait thirty days, thereby delaying the purchase. During that month, find two other items that are similar and compare prices. If it's still available at a good price and it fits the next month's budget, then buy it. What I think you'll find is you're buying less because this delay gives you the opportunity to get beyond the impulse.

Make it your policy to never use credit cards for impulse purchases. As a matter of fact, it's best to leave your credit cards at home. Don't even carry them to the mall or to the store. I'll take this impulse buying detonation process one step further—don't shop. Hightail it on out of the mall and the stores, for that's where the majority of impulse purchases occur in the first place. If you ain't there, you can't buy it, cowboy.

Still More Budget Busters

The final area that busts budgets is gifts. These items can blow up an entire budget very fast. Think about the gifts you buy for relatives, teachers, baby showers, weddings, birthdays, Valentine's Day, Mother's Day, Father's Day, kids' birthdays, and anniversaries. In the military we also have welcome gifts, farewells, pin-on, hospitality...and the list goes on for both of us. This doesn't even cover the biggie—Christmas.

The first thing we should do is evaluate the "why" of gift-giving. Do we really have to give a material gift in each circumstance? Wouldn't a card work just as well in some cases? What about baked goods instead? Occasionally, the giving of a gift puts the other person under a sense of obligation. Are you putting more emphasis on the "gift" rather than the "giver"? Isn't it, after all, the thought that counts?

One of the ways to save on gifts is to make or bake some of them. I value handmade gifts because I know the time and effort that goes into them. I only handcraft a few special gifts for very special people— because my time is also a gift. All my welcome and hospitality gifts are baked goods. I've yet to have someone turn up their nose at a hot loaf of honey whole wheat bread made from freshly ground wheat flour as a hospitality present.

Children can earn money for the gifts they give and learn the value of a dollar in the process. You don't have to keep up with the neighbors and buy the latest video game for your son's classmate at school. Often the simple board games or educational toys afford the most playing hours.

I keep a calendar of special events and dates. If I'm making a cross-stitch or other craft for that special day, then marking the start time/complete time of the project on my calendar helps. Gathering the gifts that need to be mailed in advance of the special day helps avoid a priority postage charge. As a matter of fact, I usually mail most of my Christmas gifts the day after Thanksgiving—which brings us to our bonus tip.

Bonus Tip—Christmas Budget/Stress Buster

It's the most wonderful time of the year, or so the song goes. Yet why do we have so much stress and insanity during this season? Christmas can be a major budget buster. It only takes a few short days to wipe out an entire year's worth of diligence.

Thinking about the spirit of Christmas every day of the year helps during the hectic season. It reminds us to prepare throughout the year—thereby minimizing the stress of the holidays and the expense. Here are some pre-holiday tips.

Buy on December 26. Christmas paper, bows, cards, decorations, and nonperishable gifts. Think about those items that will store well and invest accordingly. One season, I bought enough (incredibly cute) gift bags (at 90 percent off retail) to last five years! The entire bag investment was only $10.

Buy year-round. Try to think Christmas all year-round and shop the clearance aisles and loss leaders. These expenses are absorbed into our monthly budget, and we get the benefit of sales and clearance prices on gifts.

Photo greeting cards. We have photos made in October and get the savings of an early-bird discount on photo greeting cards. By writing an annual Christmas letter in the middle of November and addressing the envelopes before Thanksgiving, the cards can go out the day after Thanksgiving. We save ourselves the stress of that task during the height of the busy holiday. An added benefit is that people are more likely to actually *read* that holiday letter if it's one of the first they receive.

Bake ahead of time. Baked goods are the standard Kay family gift to neighbors. We try to get this baking done around the first of December and deliver these goods early. I make items that freeze well and can be baked in several portions. For example, banana bread and pumpkin bread are baked in coffee cans, and they freeze well. By making four coffee can loaves instead of two regular-size loaves, I have a quick gift as close as my freezer. Tie a pretty bow around it or some raffia, add a photo greeting card, and you have a yummy personalized gift.

Deliver early. We bake a loaf of bread for each of the children's teachers. That includes Sunday school, educational, and extracurricular teachers. Bob and I reason that they invest in our children's lives on a regular basis, and we don't want them forgotten in the midst of the holidays. Some years, I'll make a simple ornament with the child's picture on it. I make this ornament out of a mini grapevine wreath wrapped with holiday ribbon. We center the child's photo on the wreath and trace a circle on the photo. After the child cuts the circle out, we glue it to the wreath and attach a ribbon on back to hang it with. Or I buy the plastic ornament frames at 50 percent off at the previous year's after-Christmas sales.

This past Christmas, I gave away twenty-five loaves of bread, but I only made the photo ornaments for our annual family collection. You might even want to let your children help in the baking.

Three Gifts. Part of the Kay Family Simplification Plan involves the number of gifts each of our children receives. I'll never forget one Christmas before I had children. I watched a little boy get so many gifts that he got tired of opening them and quit. He was spoiled by his parents and both sets of grandparents and thought Christmas was all about him.

We limit the gifts to three per child, since that's how many gifts the wise men gave baby Jesus. We've decided—if it's good enough for Jesus, then it's good enough for us. The gifts are selected carefully, paying special attention to the child's requests and our budget. For example, last year Daniel got three simple gifts: a new computer, a television, and a VCR. (Just kidding.)

Actually, Daniel got a microscope (purchased at 50 percent off), a favorite video (from a warehouse club), and a handheld video game (a store's loss leader). He was pleased, and since we bought these things throughout the year, they didn't break our budget. We buy the same way for birthdays and other special holidays.

Wonder Woman Wanna-be

Tips to Cutting Yourself Some Slack

As a girl, I watched Lynda Carter in the television series *Wonder Woman*. She could pull out her gold rope and lasso any villain that got in her way. She jumped over life's obstacles without letting her little costume fall off—a feat worthy of superhero status. As a former "Miss World," Lynda had the perfect body, perfect boyfriend (although he was a *tiny bit* one-dimensional), and perfect hairstyle. Having never missed an episode—I was a certifiable Wonder Woman Wanna-be. You can imagine my reaction upon the discovery that she was a myth. My childish attitude was one of extreme disappointment. *You mean a woman can't break through a brick wall and never mess up her hair? You mean that secretary with the black horn-rimmed glasses won't turn into a beauty when she hears of trouble in paradise? You mean the average woman has thighs bigger than Lynda Carter's waist?*

There's another female who reminds me of Wonder Woman. She's found in Proverbs 31 and is called "the virtuous woman." Listen to some of the things she does.

An excellent wife, who can find? For her worth is far above jewels. The heart of her husband trusts in her and he will have no lack of gain. She does him good and not evil all the days of her life. She looks for wool and flax, and works with her hands in delight. She is like merchant ships; she brings her food from afar. She rises also while it is still night, and gives food to her household, and portions to her maidens. She considers a field and buys it; from her earnings she plants a vineyard. She girds herself with strength, and makes her arms strong. She senses that her gain is good; her lamp does not go out at night. She stretches out her hands to the distaff, and her hands grasp the spindle. She extends her hand to the poor; and she stretches out her hands to the needy. She is not afraid of the snow for her household, for all her household are clothed with scarlet. She makes coverings for herself; Her clothing is fine linen and purple... (NASB).

You might want to read the entire passage, because it goes on to describe this woman's impressive résumé—it's quite the list. Since I'm a person who makes, checks, and keeps lists, I decided I would see how I measured up on the virtuous woman list. Let's look at the last passage from the previous paragraph: "Her clothing is fine linen and purple." I got a great purple linen suit at the thrift shop for $7, so I can dress like this woman of virtue. So what if it's a size 8 and I can't unbutton the jacket because my waistline hangs over the waistband? Who needs to unbutton a jacket in the North Country, anyway?

Also included is the verse, "She is like merchant ships; she brings her food from afar." I can do that. Teaching men and women to be merchants when they consider a purchase is my business. In addition, I drive all the way downtown to get my food sometimes—that's pretty far.

Let's look at the line "She extends her hand to the poor." Helping the poor, well, that's one of the main points of this book. *She rises while it is still dark.* Yeah, I do that—when Conan wets his bed. *She girds herself with strength.* Hey! Going to the gym is a regular part of my week.

I may be good at lists, but, as Yenta (chapter 1) would say—*such a list!* When all these are wrapped in a pretty package and then lived out—well, I must confess, I fail. To be perfectly honest, I fail big time.

After all, if Wonder Woman is a legend, then isn't the virtuous woman also a myth? Not really. Still, the way I read Proverbs 31, I've got to ask, "Shouldn't she be called 'the *virtually impossible* woman'?" Who can live up to that standard? There was a time when I was tempted to give up on Miss V the same way I gave up on Miss World all those years ago.

The day I realized this proverbial standard could not be kept was a day that will live in infamy. I was taking a class on the management of human resources. My own human resources weren't being managed very well—so I'd learn how to manage someone else's. On that morning, five-year-old

Daniel climbed a forty-foot pine tree and wouldn't come down for the baby-sitter. Bob was, of course, out on assignment. The sitter called me at school, pulled me out of class, and I rushed home to find Daniel riding his bike.

At lunch, three-year-old Philip ran off to join the postal service. He was pulled out of the mail truck just before he committed a federal crime—destroying the mail. Later that afternoon, two-year-old Bethany climbed on top of Bob's dresser, pulled his Air Force Academy sword off the wall, and used it as a walking stick—pointed side up. Thankfully, I retrieved it before she was hurt.

The Kay guardian angels were working overtime and so was Mom. The angels succeeded, but I felt like a failure. My children couldn't be stopped from climbing trees, harassing the postman, or endangering their lives. That forty-foot tree began to look like an attractive hideout. No, that wouldn't work. They'd find me around dinnertime.

In the midst of these circumstances, how could I possibly keep the virtuous woman list?

That evening I wearily pulled on my T-shirt with the slogan: "I am woman. I am invincible. I am tired." What I needed was a "pick me up." Putting on the coffee, I started to raid the cupboards for chocolate.

Crawling up on the kitchen countertop made me wonder, *Why do I always hide these on the uppermost shelves?* Grumbling was a regular part of feeling sorry for myself. At that moment, the Great Chocolate Search was interrupted by singing. It was my little songbird of a girl coming into the kitchen. She sang dramatically, "I like to eat de potato chips. But Papaaaa...he got dem first and ate dem all up." Verses two through twenty went much the same way. While getting down from the counter, I fondly watched my little blond "bunny" girl and thought, *She is so incredibly precious.*

That's when it happened. There was no bolt of lightning, no burning bush—there wasn't even a UPS truck. Nonetheless, God sent me a message—through a singing telegram. A still, small voice spoke to my heart. *Ellie, you are just as precious to Me. The way you see your little girl is the way I see you.* Gradually, my self-pity was replaced by incredible comfort.

It occurred to me that *God does not require perfection, only perseverance.* The sight of Bethany hopping through her day, making up songs came to mind. God looked upon me with the same sense of affection. In my busy day of mothering, God saw me and smiled. My failed attempts to keep the children from trees and mail trucks didn't matter. He still loves me because I am

Beloved of God. He places no requirements on performance. There's no conditional acceptance on His part. He thinks I'm precious, and He thinks I'm cute.

So I keep trying.

Maybe you don't experience these kinds of frustrations. Maybe you've never suffered from low self-esteem, depression, or the pressure of "I just can't do it all." If you've never struggled with any of these things, then you're dead (at worst) or a liar (at best). On the other hand, you could be one of those incredibly together people who had a perfect childhood and has few faults. In which case, I should be reading *your* book.

It is human to struggle. It's natural to battle the pressures of the world around us. You are not alone. But there's one thing you need to keep in mind. God has a plan for you, even in the midst of a honey-covered kitchen floor.

It helps to remember you're Beloved of God, and that He is not as concerned with perfection as He is with perseverance. So carry on, my friend, and cut yourself some slack.

Tips to Cutting Yourself Some Slack

Happiness Is a Choice

As you've probably seen by now, there's not a lot of control over the specifics in my life. Some people don't like my smile—I can't help that. Nor can I change the fact that my feet are ugly. My children make their own choices that I try to influence but cannot absolutely control. Unfortunately, the timing on Señor Mischief's next mess is an unknown factor. No one has complete control over their future. Bob doesn't know where the air force will send our family next. Bethany House Publishers doesn't know how many copies of this book they'll sell. I don't know when I'll meet a grocery store clerk having a bad-hair day.

We can *influence* our next assignment—to a point. The publishers and I can work together to try and generate book sales. I can even tell the grumpy cashier a story—to help her smile. But when you get right down to it, there are too many circumstances over which you and I have no control.

On the other hand, everyone has a choice in regard to their *response* to circumstances. We can't control the kind of childhood we had (and some of you had horrible, no good, very bad childhoods), but we can choose our response today. I've heard it said that life is 10 percent circumstance and 90 percent attitude—and I agree. Sure, we all have bad days when we run for the chocolate stash. But with God's help, we can choose to be content because often happiness is a choice.

Sanity Check

Do you know a great way to cut yourself some slack? Talk to other people in the same circumstance and realize you're not alone. If you're a mother of preschoolers, then join a local MOPS group. (Call 1-303-733-5353 for the MOPS group nearest you.) If you're a military spouse, gather with your military friends and compare stories. I'm not talking about a gripe session here—those are rarely productive and only serve to foster bad feelings. I'm talking about a safe place (among people of similar background) to help you feel valued, encouraged, and accepted.

I've usually been involved in some kind of Bible study for the last fifteen years, and they have been my sanity check. Sure, some studies are better than others. The important factor is time spent learning more about this God who loves and accepts me—and wants me to be sane.

Learn to Laugh

It's important to laugh—that's a recurring theme in this book. You know what? It's also important to learn how to laugh *at yourself*. I knew a young woman years ago, who I'll call Cynthia. She was a sweet girl who had one of those no good, very bad childhoods. Then she married a man very much like her father and had a terrible, no good, very bad marriage. I encouraged her to go to counseling for a while. Largely due to her choices, she emerged from her circumstance as a *victor* rather than a *victim*.

I was amazed when Cynthia told me what she believed to be the key phrase used by her counselor that made the difference in her emotional healing. This wise man (with fifteen years' experience) told her, "You know how I'll know you're getting better, Cynthia? I'll know you're getting better when you can learn to laugh at yourself." Now she's one of the best sources of a belly laugh that I have at my disposal. She's learned to see the upside of the bad side—her circumstances have made her better, not bitter. And finally, she's learned to laugh at herself.

Laughing at yourself is a great way to cut yourself some slack. As I've said before, I believe that you either learn to look at life in a funny way—or you end up on a funny farm.

Take a Nap

In her book *Mom on the Run,* Nancy Kennedy has a chapter with a wonderful title moms can relate to. It's called "Night Night, Sleep Tight (Yeah, Right)" (Sisters, Ore.: Multnomah Books, 1996, p. 115). You can guess what the chapter talks about—a mother's inalienable right to sleep-deprivation. Cut yourself some slack by taking a nap when the kids nap. Or get to bed at a decent hour (like 7:30 P.M.), and I don't mean drool on the couch while watching *Wheel of Fortune* either. Taking care of yourself means getting enough rest to recharge for the adventure-packed days ahead.

I Dun't Know

When my friend Donna and I watched reruns of *I Love Lucy,* we loved Ricky Ricardo's accent—especially when he said, "I dun't know." Being the exceptionally mature teenagers we were, we made a game of the line. I'd ask her a dumb question like, "How much is one plus one?" Donna would answer, "I dun't know." Then Donna would ask, "Who's buried in Grant's tomb?" I'd answer, "I dun't know." My favorite question was, "How many days can Ellie stay on a diet without cheating?"

As adults, we can learn a lot from our teenage years. Sometimes, as *the* wife, *the* mother, *the* adult, *the* supervisor, *the* professional—we feel we *have* to know it all. But the refreshing, slack-cutting truth is—*we don't always have to have an answer.* That's why people write books and give classes and lectures. There's help out there when we don't have the answer for a problem.

Of course, we have to be careful about the kind of help we seek. There are so-called "answers" readily available on television talk shows, soap operas, and in sensationalistic magazines. But are these sources consistent with our core values? Springer—chairs flying through the air? Need I say more?

You can find resources that *are* consistent with your values. First, however, you have to admit, "I dun't know." Personally, I learned a lot early in my marriage by listening to Christian radio shows such as *Focus on the Family, Through the Bible Hour, Insight for Living,* and *Manna for Today.* While I was cleaning, cooking, or crafting, I'd listen to the radio—turned up full blast—and absorb all that instructional material. My neighbors may have learned a few things, too.

Run With It

Are you a mom who works inside the home? If you are, then you're one of the people most likely to need some slack. The main reason you won't cut yourself any is because you're home. So much more is expected. After all, you have all this extra *time,* right? There's a unique advantage to being a full-time-in-the-home employee, one that isn't often mentioned. What is this special stay-at-home perk? I'm glad you asked.

I'll let Brenda Hunter, Ph.D., a woman with a complete brain, answer that question. In *Home by Choice,* she wrote, "A mother at home has the opportunity to expand her horizons, take a talent, and run with it. As a corporate executive has said, 'Any man who works forty or sixty-plus hours per week and commutes has little time, after functioning as husband and father, to pursue his own interests.' The woman at home has that privilege" (Sisters, Ore.: Multnomah Books, 1991, p. 132).

If you like to clip coupons, develop a seminar. If you enjoy garage sales, then write a book. If you're a good listener, talk to the waitress having a difficult day. If you have the gift of gab, cheer up people at a retirement home. If you're good at crafts, teach your half-witted neighbor how to make a fabric box, or sell them at a craft fair. Take that interest or talent and run with it.

Find a Kindred Spirit

My bosom friend, Brenda, loves me more than a sister, and she shows it on a regular basis. Madeline has fanned the flame of my dream when the embers of disappointment threaten to extinguish all hope. Loretta has given me perspective in the midst of great rejection. Maurveen and Pauline have prayed for me as only a mother in the Lord can, with consistency and tender compassion. All these women know the real Ellie Kay—and it ain't all purty. Despite such knowledge, they love me anyway.

In my opinion, factors that set apart a *kindred spirit* from a *friend* are connection and acceptance. The ladies mentioned *connect* intellectually, emotionally, relationally, and *spiritually.* They cut me slack by telling me the truth in love. Since I know they *accept* me, I can hear the truth from them, even when it ain't purty. They have the ability to do this because they spend time in the source of truth—the Bible.

If you find a kindred spirit, cultivate that relationship. If you're not already married, marry a kindred spirit—like I did. My Beloved builds me up when the world blows my dream full of holes; he tenderly caresses wounded emotions when I've been betrayed; and reminds me that I don't have to be perfect to be accepted.

Creative Giving

Tips to Finding Organizations That Love Your Donations

A lady named Cindy attended one of my seminars. One Saturday afternoon she was traveling down Main Street in her town. In the car trunk she had four bags of groceries (for which she'd only paid ten dollars). When she stopped for a lady in a crosswalk, she noticed the woman was blind and assisted by her four young children. They pushed a metal cart with one small bag of groceries, and Cindy assumed they had come from the supermarket.

A still, small voice spoke to her heart and said, *Stop your car and give them your groceries.* She'd *never* had any thoughts like this before and didn't know how to respond.

It must have been the pizza I had for lunch, she thought.

Again, the impression was clear. *Give them all of your groceries. You can make the choice to obey or not. It's your blessing to have or refuse.*

She turned her car around, found the young family, and ran to them with the groceries in her arms. As she placed the bags in the lady's metal cart she said, "I know you don't know me and that's not important. What is important is that you know that God loves you and He wants you to have these groceries."

The woman was bewildered and overcome by the kindness of a stranger. As Cindy walked away, she heard the children exclaim, "Look Mama, there's milk, fruit, and even GUM!"

The woman stood on the sidewalk, sobbing, "Thank you! Oh,

thank you!"

While Cindy was in the store earlier that day, saving money and using coupons, God had another woman in mind. As she purchased milk, juice, and gum, He was providing through her for four young children and their blind mother.

God's care for those in need is the Christian perspective in action. His provision for *you* individually and *your* need is the message of the *Share* portion of *Shop, Save, and Share.*

But it doesn't stop there: God will also allow you the joy of giving to His children out of your abundance. That's what makes this message so unique.

If you give yourself to the hungry,
and satisfy the desire of the afflicted, then your light
will rise in darkness, and your gloom will become like midday.
Isaiah 58:10

Tips to Finding Organizations That Love Your Donations
Mission of Joy

Your purchase of this book helps children in an underdeveloped country because a portion of the proceeds from *Shop, Save, and Share* go to support the Mission of Joy. While *many* people espouse a Christian philosophy, few will venture to help a neighbor. When I meet a person who talks the talk *and* also walks the walk—I have to pay attention.

The O'Leary family's commitment to giving makes you take notice.

Jeff is a career military officer who went on a mission trip to India in 1990 along with fellow air force officer Mike Krueger. These families were so moved by the Indian people's need for food, clothing, and shelter that they put their money (and time) where their mouth was—and founded Mission of Joy (MOJ).

That same year, Jeff and Mike provided the financial resources to open the first orphanage in India in a rented house with fifteen children. Today, they support more than one hundred and forty children in four orphanages. Additionally, they have built dozens of village churches and sponsor forty-four native missionaries (and their families) who serve in dozens of MOJ-sponsored areas.

Jeff and his wife, Cindy, say this is just a "drop in the ocean of needs in India." In their many trips to India (at their own expense) they have seen people who live on one or two bowls of rice a day—and it is enough. Jeff's Christian worldview in action is: "I believe my purpose in life is greater than increasing my standard of living—greater than finding a way to eat or drink better. I want to do something of eternal value. When we put God first, He begins to change our hearts as well as our financial circumstances. My heart doesn't desire the things that would consume our finances and keep me from giving back abundantly to God. He has taken away my desire for the 'toys' in this world and replaced it with a stronger desire to store up eternal joy in His kingdom by sharing myself, my time, and my resources."

As the O'Learys have sacrificed the "extras" that many of their peers say are essential, they've seen God provide abundantly for their needs and for the orphans in India. Cindy and Jeff have four children of their own, and they raised two other abandoned children to adulthood. Cindy has remained home as a full-time homemaker during this entire time. They've also seen God provide for their children's college needs through scholarships and work/study programs. Their son Stephen is a premed student with an eye to serving someday as a doctor in India.

The entire staff at Mission of Joy is volunteer. They keep their monthly expenses at a minimum so they can send the maximum to where the needs are greatest—India. During its existence, MOJ has sent *97 percent* of all contributions directly to India. Ask any nonprofit organization—that's an amazing percentage. While MOJ does not spend advertising dollars soliciting funds, they do believe in sharing their needs. In doing so they've seen God provide, through people like you and me, for so many in such desperate need.

Mission of Joy will provide an Indian child with food, clothing, and education for a donation of $25 per month. You can contact Mission of Joy at P.O. Box 39593, Tacoma, WA 98439. If you want to learn more about the history and current status of MOJ, visit them on the WorldWide Web site at www.missionjoy.org.

The American Red Cross (ARC)

This humanitarian organization, led and governed by volunteers, is dedicated to helping and preparing American people to cope with emergencies. During the ice storm our local ARC chapter organized the community effort to provide shelter and assistance to victims of this natural disaster. Check your Yellow Pages for the organization nearest you.

Many ARC chapters serve as a collection point for food donations. They will forward these groceries to a community food pantry. Financial donations go to help one of their many programs such as biomedical services, disaster services, and community and international services. They have regular blood drives for those who want to donate this life-giving resource. *Kiplinger's Personal Finance* and *Money* magazines have consistently rated the Red Cross as one of the top five U.S. charities in their annual reviews.

Contributions can be mailed to your local Red Cross chapter, to ARC, P.O. Box 37423, Washington, DC 20013, or you may call 1-800-HELP-NOW. Donations can also be made through the Internet site at www.redcross.org.

Homeless Shelters

The volunteers who work these shelters are truly are on the front lines of fighting hunger. These groups welcome not only your food and clothing but your time as well. There's nothing like a day serving soup to make a family thankful for the food they eat inside comfortable homes.

Our family tries to help homeless people when we see them on the street holding a sign that says, "Will work for food." While we don't feel comfortable giving money that could possibly go to support addictive behavior or a self-seeking lifestyle (some "professional" homeless folks make up to $50 an hour), we still want to do *something*.

At age nine, Daniel, our oldest, came up with the idea of keeping canned goods in the console of the Suburban. Now we hand them two cans of chili or pasta meals. When we first started doing this, the children were so eager to give to the homeless—that they tried to find them on the street.

"THERE'S A HOMELESS MAN!" shouted Philip as he pointed to a man by the side of the road.

I looked where Philip was pointing and saw a young man on a bicycle. For the third time that day I said, "Philip, that is not a homeless man. He's on a bicycle and his blue jeans are just dirty—he doesn't even have a sign!"

Disappointed, Philip shrugged. "Well, he looked kind of lost to me.

Maybe we could give him some clothes soap."

It's the heart attitude that counts.

The Local Church

Personally, Bob and I choose to give 10 percent of our gross income to our local church. We've done this for the last fifteen years—it's a part of our monthly budget. Some people call this practice a "tithe," others call it foolish, but we call it Christianity in practice.

Every church can be a distribution point of groceries to those in need. While many churches have organized clothing closets, food pantries, food drives, and stocked kitchens, such organization is not a prerequisite. If you want to give goods to a family in need, ask your church to be a distribution point for you. Their part can be as involved as a deacon's visit to deliver the food to people, or as simple as a secretary's phone call to the needy family to arrange a pickup of the items. Either way, keep a record of your donations for tax purposes and a "no tab" attitude in your heart.

There are many people who fit into this church's scope of assistance. They include those in financial need due to an illness or loss of employment, as well as those in need of cooked meals—the shut-ins, a brand-new mom, or ministry groups passing through town.

Some churches are diverse in their distribution. Our church in New Mexico, Christ Community Church, gave groceries to all those listed above plus contributions to orphanages in Mexico, a local children's home, a crisis pregnancy center, and a battered women's shelter. You might even want to volunteer to organize your church's food pantry.

Crisis Pregnancy Centers

These centers provide assistance to women in crisis pregnancies. They give tangible help to women through the distribution of maternity clothes, toiletries, diapers, formula, baby food, and groceries. Look up your nearest center in the local phone book.

Orphanages and Children's Homes

Call your local children's home and ask for a "needs list." Often these lists are very specific due to the age, gender, and size of their children, as well as nutrition and health requirements. They welcome your assistance whether they are located in the United States or in another country.

Women's Shelters

Women and children who seek these shelters often come for help with only the clothes on their backs. These shelters especially need trial-size toiletries, as their occupants may stay for a day or for a year. Look in the Yellow Pages under "spouse abuse" for the phone number. Don't be surprised if you are asked to drop off the needed items at an office downtown rather than the home itself—confidentiality is necessary for adequate occupant protection.

During a six-month period, I got thirty-five bottles of hair coloring free with my couponing. These were donated to this shelter with the understanding that the women could exchange them in the local grocery store for the right shade. Sometimes it's the little things that make the difference in a difficult situation.

Postal Workers' Food Drives

Every year postal workers collect millions of pounds of nonperishable foods for people in need. In addition, there are Boy Scout/Girl Scout food drives and others throughout the community. A seminar graduate, Brenda Conway, said she used to donate a can or two to her children's scout food drives. Now she donates two bags of goods per child.

First Sergeant's Pantry/Community Food Pantries

Because we are a military family, I am acquainted with this organization's assistance to military families in need. Some of the younger troops are attempting to serve our country and feed their families on a salary so low they qualify for government assistance. Call your local military installation and ask them about this pantry.

There are also other church and civic organizations that have food pantries. If every family reading this book gave just three canned good items per week—there would be no hungry families in our communities.

The Salvation Army and Goodwill Industries

These nonprofit groups help support disabled Americans through the provision of jobs. Be sure to drop off your donations during business hours so you can secure a tax-deductible receipt. They also help provide clothing to third-world organizations. The amount of clothing they've sent overseas in the last twenty years could fill 30,000 Sam's stores! That's a good amount of cotton.

Basically, we can help anyone in need. Throughout this book you've read accounts of ordinary people helping others in extraordinary ways. If we look around us and pull off our blinders, we'll find people who long for a kindhearted act of compassion.

Potty Water Principles

Twenty Phantoms

R est. What a nice thought, a great concept. Rest is hard for a woman who wears many hats.

I awake by 5:30 A.M., put on my mommy hat, and hit the floor running. Feeding babies, dressing babies, and loving babies. Next comes on my maid hat, and I clean the messes babies make. It requires hard work. Who has time for rest? I try to rest during my lunch break with one of six daily glasses of water. Usually, I try to sit in the living room and eat my meal after the children have had their lunches. During this hallowed time, the babies are napping and the older children are having a quiet time.

As a special treat, I'll sip a glass of *tea* while trying to grab a few minutes of relaxation. Eternal vigilance requires that I pick up my glass of water or tea afterward, lest the babies awaken and try to drink it—more likely, *spill* it.

One day, I put on a lady of leisure hat and "rested" with a rare glass of tea. I was busy when three-year-old Señor Mischief and his one-year-old protégé awoke from their naps. Panicked, I remembered my unsupervised tea. Grabbing my emergency hat, I quickly checked it...*whew!*...the glass was undisturbed. But it was puzzling to see *water* in it. *That's funny, I thought I was drinking tea.*

There was a vague memory of my pouring water earlier in the day, so I dismissed my confusion as typical half-witted forgetfulness (my Beloved calls it premature senility). That water looked good, so I decided to finish it in a big gulp. Yuk!! This was *not* the purified water we drink! At that moment, confusion reigned because the babies were fighting again, so I put on my referee hat and ran to the boys' room.

After removing Conan the Baby Barbarian's hands from Sweetpea's neck, Jonathan announced, "Mama, I help with your tea...I pour it out."

Envisioning tea stains on the bed quilt I asked, "Where did you pour it out, Sweetpea?"

He squared his shoulders and proudly replied, "In de bafroom."

"*Where* in the bathroom?" My inquiring mind wanted to know.

His reply brought a sigh of relief as he sweetly answered, "In de sink."

My relief was short-lived, for there was more to his story. "And I get you water," he said, beaming with pride.

Nervously looking at the empty glass on the end table I asked, "And where did you get the water?"

"In the bafroom," he answered with confidence.

Still hopeful, there was one last question ventured. "Out of the sink?"

"No!" he replied as if he thought I was out of my mind. "Out of de potty, Mama. Der's lots of water in the potty!"

I sprayed my mouth with Lysol. The motto of this anecdote: When at the Kays', DON'T DRINK THE WATER!

The Potty Water Principle

There's another lesson learned from Jonathan's water—things are not always what they seem. Purified water looks like potty water, even to an expert. People are a lot like water: they look alike on the outside, but the difference lies within.

On the outside, the grocery store checker looks to be having an average day at her regular job. But inside she could be experiencing the agony of rejection. To the casual observer I may appear to be a confident seminar presenter. But at times, I experience self-doubt and question the choices I've made. Only God knows our hidden selves.

The good news is, God not only knows us, He wants us to know more about *Him.* He wants to give us the ultimate exchange—better than unlimited triple coupons every day of the week. I'm reminded of the television series *Touched by an Angel.* It portrays God's involvement in our lives—especially in the midst of problems. There's always a moment of truth at the end of each episode when one of the angels looks at a human being and says, "You see, God loves you." That's the message of this chapter—God loves *you*.

He knows all about the potty water you've sipped, and He wants to give you something better—much better. Have you ever felt a longing deep inside for something *more*? Have you ever wondered if God could truly care about someone like you? Each of us is born with a God-longing. We want to find truth. We want to discover the ultimate reality. We all want that empty question in our hearts answered. The answer is found in the topic of water.

When it comes to water, I know a man who could have given the Culligan man a run for his money. This man was in the business of taking potty water and making it pure. Just ask a Samaritan woman from the book of John in the Bible. (Yeah, right, Ellie. We're supposed to ask some woman who lived 2,000 years ago!) Hey, it could happen.

This woman knew about rejection; she knew what it meant to be afraid, and she knew what it meant to be labeled. When she met the water guy, she thought he was just another man—like the bug guy or the Maytag repairman. Just another man—she'd seen plenty (and I do mean *plenty*). She'd been married five times and was living with prospect number six. She knew a little something about guys—or so she thought.

This water man was different—*very different*. Unlike the other men from the area, this one looked at her as if he could see the years of pain she'd been through. He knew everything there was to know about her— he even knew the names she was called. He knew what she was and he knew why. All of this in just one look.

Rumors like to fly in a town like hers. Some guys knew her history by word of mouth, and others knew from experience. All had turned their backs on her. She was used to it. The women...well, that was another story entirely. The women of her village wrote the book on rejection—they made sure everyone treated her as an outcast. She'd feel the bitter sting of their judgment until a new love came along. He'd help fill the empty spot in her heart—for a while. Another man, another relationship, another breakup. She'd been there, done that.

This water guy was different. He knew her past and her present, for that matter—but He didn't judge her. He looked at her with—could it be? He looked at her with *compassion*. Those religious folks judged her; she could never measure up to their standards. She was too far gone for that.

She'd heard this guy was religious, too. He was a great teacher, a rabbi in a nation of people who thought her kind of people were—well, half-breeds. Yet He didn't treat her like a half-breed. He was actually kind. He was also generous.

He told her about the radical water He gives—living water. She would never have to thirst again. If she accepted His water, she could find healing from the despair of her past. She discovered a peace she'd never known. She could stop running—and hurting. So can you.

The Prayer Principle

I met a woman in 1992 when I presented the *Shop, Save, and Share* Seminar at the Mothers of Preschoolers (MOPS) international convention. After one of the workshops, this woman approached me with an incredible story. She was a lot like the Samaritan woman—on the run, but for a different reason. She was a typical shopper, running to the store several times a week for the things she needed. Her husband thought she was spending too much money on food and asked her to add up all of the "little trips" to the store. To her astonishment, she spent $750 each month to feed her family of four. The average family of four spent $494 a month on food that year. (*Food Economic Review,* R. Blaylock, and D. M. Smallwood, Washington, D.C., 1992).

She did not serve filet mignon. Nor did she entertain the church choir with a banquet. She didn't even feed teenage boys—but two preschoolers. She knew drastic changes were needed, and so she did something radical. She didn't apply organizational tips or start providing for the poor—she turned to prayer.

The next month, her food budget went down to $300. After the seminar, she trimmed another 30 percent off her grocery bill, for a total of $210. The reason for both reductions is very simple: Prayer works.

Here's an example of one woman's prayer over her food budget:

Dear Lord,
You know how I've been doing on my food budget. I've never even been on a budget before, and I've certainly never given this area of my life over to you. But I'm doing that now. I don't want it anymore. I don't want the responsibility; I'm sick of it. It's yours now; I

commit my budget to you. Really! Please help me. You know in my heart I want to. Also, help me not to be afraid.
Amen.

When I shoot up an arrow prayer on the way to the grocery store, it's uncanny how the things I need just happen to be on sale and I have a double or triple coupon for them. "Pray before you shop" is the motto to adopt.

We don't have to limit our prayers to shopping, either. God really cares and hears your prayer. Every now and then we just have to remind ourselves to listen.

> The mind of man plans his way,
> but the Lord directs his steps.
> Proverbs 16:9

The Principle of Priorities

My husband, Bob, does not subscribe to the philosophy "Jack of all trades and master of none." He is a master of many things—fathering, communicating, fighter-piloting, and buffeting. You may not have heard of that last skill on the list...nonetheless, he's a master of it.

Buffeting is the art of piling items on a plate while on a "one trip through" buffet line. Bob piles it so high that the food often falls onto the floor. After he gets through the salad, rolls, vegetables, and main course, he has no room for dessert. I don't tell him his buffeting talent is embarrassing. Instead, I'll say, "Beloved, why don't you go ahead and go through the line by yourself. I'll wait at the table with the children and take my turn later." Much later. It works every time.

Life is like a buffet line in many ways. There are a lot of good things available to put on our plate: helping in the children's classrooms, volunteer work, working outside the home, choir, exercising, etc. We keep piling things higher and higher until we don't have room for dessert.

Our goal is to eliminate some of the *good* things on our plates so we have room for the *best*. This brings us to another aspect of prayer—asking God about His *priorities* in our lives. Women today have so many demands on their time and energies. Adding one *more* thing can seem overwhelming. Precisely the reason we need God's direction and wisdom. James 1:5 gives us the assurance that God *will* give us guidance.

This is not a wish or a hope; it is a done deal—a promise.

> But if any of you lacks wisdom, let him ask of God, who
> gives to all men generously and without reproach,
> and it will be given him.
> James 1:5

The Phantom Principle

Not only do we need to pray about the activities that fill our lives, now is a good time to take inventory of our priorities. In their book *Building Your Mate's Self-Esteem,* Dennis and Barbara Rainey refer to a phenomenon in marriages called "phantoms."

For a number of years, my husband, Bob (aka Beloved), was an instructor pilot and taught young men to fly the F-4 Phantom. Thirty years ago, the Phantom was *the* technological wonder. It flew in low and fast. Bombs were dropped before the enemy knew the aircraft was in the area. Thus, the name "The Phantom" was given to that "manly" airplane (or so I'm told).

The Raineys define a phantom as: "An unattainable mental image or standard by which we measure our performance, abilities, looks, character, and life. It is perfect, idyllic. A phantom, by definition, is an illusion, an apparition, or a resemblance of reality."

All of us have phantoms—mental images of what we believe we should be. Think about your phantom. Take it one step further and write it on paper (or computer). Then, as James 1:5 says, ask God for *His* wisdom regarding your phantom. Let Him help you decide what to keep, what to save for later, and what to send to the trash heap.

To get you started, I'll share my phantom list:

Ellie's Top Twenty Phantoms

- My phantom is 5' 8" tall, a perfect size eight, and never has a bad-hair day.
- She runs five miles daily. As a matter of fact, she's in training for the Pikes Peak Ascent Run, which is a thirteen-mile run up a 14,000-foot mountain.
- She handmakes all her baby, wedding, birthday, hospitality, and Christmas gifts.

- She sends thirty letters to friends and family every month.
- She recycles not only newspapers and aluminum cans but cardboard, plastic, and glass, as well. Not due to financial necessity, but because of her concern for the ecology.
- Of course, she is an exceptional wife and mother who is *always* in a cheerful mood when her husband comes home from work. Even when he's late, dinner has dried in the oven, and the children have been candidates for the Mischief Hall of Fame.
- She is never irritable or short-tempered with these children.
- When administering discipline, she *always* takes Dr. Dobson's advice, making sure to balance the scales of love with justice.
- She obeys all traffic rules and never speeds, even on the rare occasion she is late for an appointment.
- She is patient and understanding with the idiots who try to run her and her babies off the road.
- She never overcommits herself socially, in ministry, or in her daily schedule. Yet she manages to fulfill every ministry opportunity that comes her way.
- She cooks a well-balanced meal each night, keeps an immaculate home, and makes her own flour, bread, cookies, cakes, and pasta.
- She homeschools her children and is a gracious hostess socially in her husband's formal functions.
- She writes well and meets her deadlines.
- She speaks with confidence in front of an audience that won't laugh at her jokes.
- The latest styles are never lost on this woman.
- She is kind to the unkind.
- She balances her time with her obligations to perfection.
- She never puts her foot in her mouth.
- And did I mention? She saves her family 85 percent on their food budget by using coupons.

As you may imagine, there are many things about my phantom that the real me will never attain. After five babies, I'll probably never see a size eight again. Also, it is impossible to refrain from overcommitment and still say yes to every opportunity that comes along. The two are mutually exclusive. You can't do it all. Wonder Woman is a myth; that series was canceled, remember? So even as I share this...don't let it become a burden, but a joy. Incorporate *Shop, Save, and Share* slowly, at your own pace.

Write out your phantom and offer it up to the Lord. Ask Him to show you what He wants you to be doing—yes, even ask Him if *He* wants you to use coupons. God will give you the wisdom you need, that's a promise.

You may have guessed it already, but the water guy we talked about earlier is God—God's Son, to be precise. And He loves you. You may want to read the book of John the next time you're in a hotel and pick up a Gideon Bible. Or maybe you have a Bible of your own, sitting on a shelf, gathering dust, waiting for you to come along.

Just like the Samaritan woman, some of you have been looking for love. This woman found her soul mate in the eyes of a Man who knew His own sorrows. She thought she understood religion. She even had her own religion—but it didn't seem to fill that empty place inside her. No man could fill that place—until she met the water guy.

May you discover, if you don't already know, that *you* are Beloved of God. He knows you by name and He's been calling you since the day you were born—Beloved.

Everyone who drinks of this water shall thirst again;
but whoever drinks of the water that I shall give him shall never thirst.
John 4:13-14

APPENDIX  A

Books and Resources

Burkett, Larry. *Your Finances in Changing Times*. Chicago, Ill.: Moody Press, 1975.

Chapman, Annie, with Maureen Rank. *Smart Women Keep it Simple*. Minneapolis, MN: Bethany House Publishers, 1997.

Dacyczyn, Amy. *The Tightwad Gazette I, II, and III*. New York: Villard Books, a division of Random House, Inc., 1996.

Freeman, Becky, and Ruthie Arnold. *Worms in My Tea and Other Kinds of Mixed Blessings*. Nashville, Tenn.: Broadman and Holman Publishers, 1991.

Freeman, Becky, and Ruthie Arnold. *Adult Children of Fairly Functional Parents*. Nashville, Tenn.: Broadman and Holman Publishers, 1993.

Freeman, Becky. *Marriage 9-1-1*. Nashville, Tenn.: Broadman and Holman Publishers, 1995.

Freeman, Becky. *Still Lickin' the Spoon*. Nashville, Tenn.: Broadman and Holman Publishers, 1997.

Freeman, Becky. *The View From the Porch Swing*. Nashville, Tenn.: Broadman and Holman Publishers, 1998.

Hunt, Mary. *The Financially Confident Woman*. Nashville, Tenn.: Broadman and Holman Publishers, 1996.

Hunt, Mary. *The Best of the Cheapskate Monthly, Simple Tips for Living Lean in the '90s*. New York: St. Martin's Press, 1993.

Hunt, Mary. *The Cheapskate Monthly Money Makeover*. New York: St. Martin's Press, 1995.

Johnson, Barbara. *Where Does a Mother Go to Resign?* Minneapolis, Minn.: Bethany House Publishers, 1994.

Lagerburg, Beth, and Mimi Wilson. *Once A Month Cooking,* re-release by Broadman and Holman Publishers, January 1999.

MacGregor, Malcolm, with Stanley C. Baldwin. *Your Money Matters.* Minneapolis, Minn.: Bethany House Publishers, updated edition, 1988.

Morgan, Elisa. *Mom to Mom.* Grand Rapids, Mich.: Zondervan Publishing House, 1996.

Partow, Donna. *Families That Play Together Stay Together.* Minneapolis, Minn.: Bethany House Publishers, 1996.

Perritt, Gerald W. *Mutual Funds Made Easy!* Chicago: Dearborn Financial Publishing, Inc., 1995.

Quinn, Jane Bryant. *Making the Most of Your Money.* New York: Simon & Schuster, 1991.

St. James, Elaine. *Simplify Your Life—100 Ways to Slow Down and Enjoy the Things That Really Matter.* New York: Hyperion, 1994.

Walker, Laura Jensen. *Dated Jekyll, Married Hyde.* Minneapolis, Minn.: Bethany House Publishers, 1997.

Yorkey, Mike. *Saving Money Any Way You Can.* Ann Arbor, Mich.: Servant Publications, 1994.

A P P E N D I X B

ACTION CHARTS			
WEEK OF:	**SHOP**	**SAVE**	**SHARE**
1/3/98	Alphabetize Coupons	Check on car insurance	Gather 3 items for bag

ACTION CHART...THIS WEEK I WILL:			
WEEK OF:	**SHOP**	**SAVE**	**SHARE**

ACTION CHART...THIS WEEK I WILL:

WEEK OF:	SHOP	SAVE	SHARE

Thank you for selecting a book from
BETHANY HOUSE PUBLISHERS

Bethany House Publishers is a ministry of Bethany Fellowship International, an interdenominational, nonprofit organization committed to spreading the Good News of Jesus Christ around the world through evangelism, church planting, literature distribution, and care for those in need. Missionary training is offered through Bethany College of Missions.

Bethany Fellowship International is a member of the National Association of Evangelicals and subscribes to its statement of faith. If you would like further information, please contact:

Bethany Fellowship International
6820 Auto Club Road
Minneapolis, MN 55438 USA